Favourite
Fish Dishes

Author: Annette Wolter
Photography: Susi and Pete Eising
Translated by UPS Translations, London
Edited by Josephine Bacon

CLB 4182
This edition published in 1995 by Colour Library Books Ltd
Published originally under the title "Fisch"
by Gräfe und Unzer Verlag GmbH, München
© 1995 Gräfe und Unzer Verlag GmbH, München
English translation copyright: © 1995 by
Colour Library Books Ltd, Godalming, Surrey
Typeset by Image Setting, Brighton, E. Sussex
Printed and bound in Singapore
All rights reserved
ISBN 1-85833-316-4

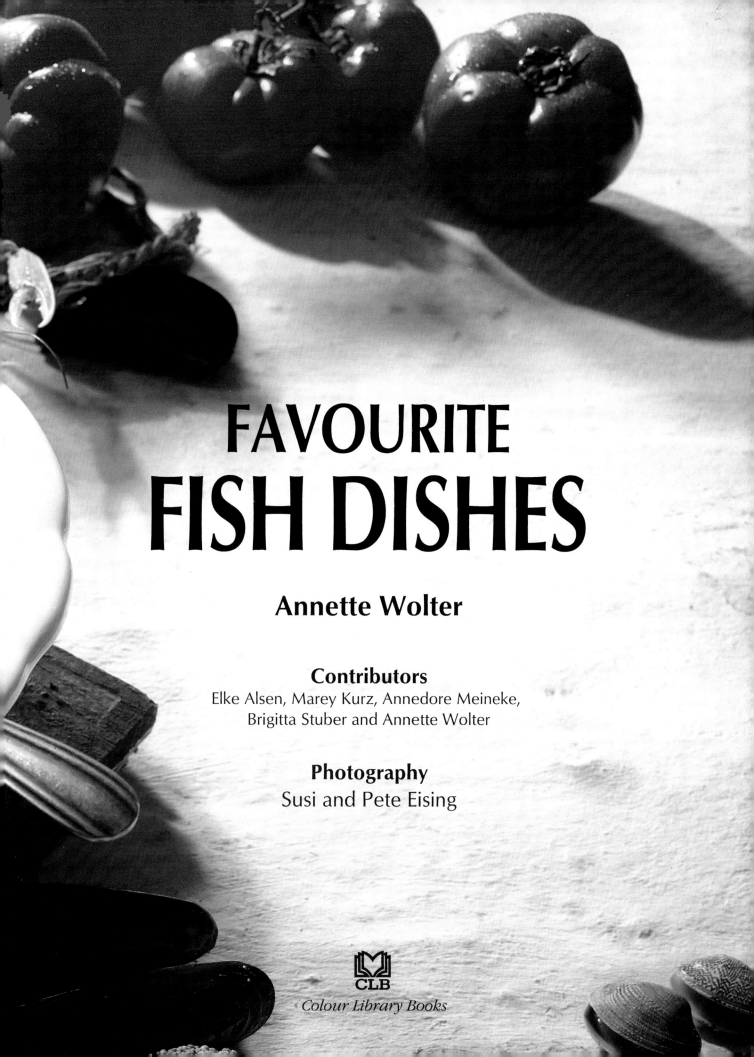

FAVOURITE
FISH DISHES

Annette Wolter

Contributors

Elke Alsen, Marey Kurz, Annedore Meineke,
Brigitta Stuber and Annette Wolter

Photography

Susi and Pete Eising

CLB

Colour Library Books

Contents

About this Book
Page 6

The Value of Fish
Page 7

Preparing Fish Correctly
Pages 8-9

Scaling 8
Cleaning 8

Skinning 8
Filleting round fish 8

Cooking Methods
Pages 10-13

Fish au bleu 10
Poaching 10
Braising 10
Steaming 10

Baking 12
Frying 12
Grilling 12
Deep frying 12

How to Eat Fish and Seafood
Pages 14-15

Fish au bleu 14
Mussels 14

Grilled scampi 15
Sole 15

Great Hors d'Oeuvres
Pages 16-41

Cold cream of crayfish
    soup 18
Classic crayfish soup 18
Cucumber and dill soup with
    shrimps 19
Cream of scampi soup with
    shrimps 19
Chinese fish soup 20
Solyanka 20

Vegetable soup with smoked
    salmon dumplings 21
Dill soup with fish
    dumplings 21
Cream of salmon soup 22
Fish soup with potatoes 22
Pea soup with shrimps 23
Cream of mussel soup 23
Barley soup with fish 24
Cream of fish soup 24
Spanish fish soup 25
French fish consommé 25
Maatjes herrings with
    mustard 26
Canapés with mackerel
    cream 26
Maatjes herring cocktail 27
Stuffed salmon rolls 27
Stuffed salmon rolls 27
Fish on cress 28
Fish crackers 28
Bloater toasts 28
Plaice rolls in green
    peppers 29

Shrimp omelettes 29
Fish soufflé with millet 30
Redfish fillet with bean
    sprouts 30
Scampi au gratin with
    cucumber 31
Vol-au-vents with shrimp
    ragoût 31
Herring fillets with spicy
    mayonnaise 32
Sweet and sour fish 33
Bass in red sauce 33
Stuffed avocados 34
Spring cocktail 34
Coley with spinach 34
Prawn cocktail 35
Shrimp cocktail 35

Lobster cocktail 35
Gravad lax 36
Smoked trout with horseradish
    sauce 36
Spiny lobster tails with
    melons 37
Special salmon mousse 38
Fish and asparagus in
    aspic 38
Scallops au gratin 39
King prawns in garlic
    butter 39
Deep-fried oysters 40
Oysters Kilpatrick 40
Oysters Rockefeller 40
Lobster au gratin 41
Lobster Dijonnaise 41

Exquisite Main Courses
Pages 42-67

Devilled cod fillets with
    broccoli and tomatoes 44
Fillet of fish Florentine 44
Fish rolls in herb sauce 45
Cuttlefish and Squid 46
Curried fish 47
Fish fricassée 47
Maatjes fillets with green
    beans 48
Halibut steaks in caper
    sauce 48
Rolled fish with sliced
    apple 49
Fish rolls in tomato sauce 49
Plaice fillets on brown
    rice 50
Trout au bleu 51
Pan-fried trout 51
Mussel ragoût in cream
    sauce 52
Shrimps in dill sauce 52
Pan-fried fish 53

Stuffed green herrings 53
Spring plaice 54
Pan-fried mackerel with
    tomatoes 54
Haddock with melted
    butter 55
Cod in wine sauce 55
Cauliflower and fish bake 56
Redfish and tomato bake 56
Stuffed rolled sole 57
Sea fish on a bed of
    vegetables 57
Fish and mussel stew 58
Norwegian fish mould 58
Waterzooi 59
Jansson's temptation 60
Matelote 60
Mussel risotto 61
Fish roulade 61
Clam chowder 62
Bouillabaisse 63
Stuffed catfish 64

Baked redfish   64
Fish au gratin   65
Chinese fish and rice   65
Arabian-style perch   66
Coley with tomatoes   67

Delicacies for Special Occasions

Pages 68-85

Fried sole with fine
      vegetables   70
Fillets of fish "tre verde"   70
Foil-baked halibut   71
Catfish in bacon   72
Trout in bacon   72
Chinese deep-fried
      scampi   73
Flambéed scampi   73
Carp oriental style   74
Polish-style carp   74
Gilt-head bream Roman
      style   75
Sea bream Tuscan style   75
Poached salmon with caviar
      sauce   76
Pike dumplings in herb
      sauce   76
Baked pike-perch   77
Pike-perch in a salt crust   78

Russian salmon pie   79
Terrine of trout   80
Char in aspic   81
Trout mousse   82
Mackerel mousse   82
Fish and vegetables in
      aspic   83
Smoked fish with tofu and
      herb mayonnaise   83
Mussels in tomato sauce   84
Mussels with mustard
      mayonnaise   84
Mexican scallops   84

Party Dishes

Pages   86-107

Fish fondue in oil   88
Fish fondue in chicken
      stock   88
Fish and potato cakes   89
Fish bread   89
Herring pie   90
Trout pâté en croûte   91
Spinach and cod flan   92
Salmon flan with cheese   92
Herrings with apples   93
Grilled pike-perch fillets   93
Grilled gilt-head bream   94
Halibut and vegetable
      brochettes with tofu   95
Plaice and scampi
      brochettes   95
Mixed grill   96
Salt herrings with
      oatmeal   97
Swedish pickled herring   97
Glassblower's herring   98
Herring in Burgundy   98
Marinated mussels   99
Maatjes-dill morsels   99
Mackerel with juniper
      berries   100
Soused herring   100
Tofu and fish with
      courgettes   101
Mackerel with
      vegetables   101
Cod cutlets in tarragon
      broth   102

Marinated haddock
      cutlets   102
Bloater salad with
      noodles   103
Mackerel and bean
      salad   103

Shrimp salad with rice   104
Shrimp and cucumber
      salad   104
Rice salad with fish   105
Bean salad with smoked
      fish   105
Dutch fish and potato
      salad   106
Astoria fish salad   107

Fine Fish Sauces

Pages   108-109
Cream and white wine
      sauce   108
Sauce Hollandaise   108

Beurre blanc   108
Sauce rémoulade   108

Recognising Fish and Shellfish

Pages 110-125

Index

Pages 126-128

About this Book

This full-colour illustrated recipe book, devoted to freshwater and sea fish, as well as shellfish, will be welcomed by lovers of fresh fish and give pleasure to all those who are aware of the health value of fish and are therefore keen to eat fish more frequently as a substitute for meat.

The recipes in this book will show you the many ways in which fish can be prepared, both on its own and in combination with other foods. The short notes attached to the recipe titles give some background to the dishes. The nutritional information giving the calorie content, protein, fat and carbohydrate content is important to those who are concerned about their diet. Calories and joules are terms in everyday use, and denote kilocalories and kilojoules.

This work is the result of collaboration between several experienced writers, and contains an especially attractive and varied range of dishes, because the authors have contributed all their best recipe ideas gleaned from years of experience and practical testing. Each dish is photographed in full colour. The recipes are described in simple language, to allow even the inexperienced to cope successfully with fish cookery. It is surprising how versatile fish can be for the most varied occasions and differing needs, and how many healthy dishes can be prepared using fish.

After a section on "The Value of Fish", the important points about fresh and frozen fish, and tips for the buying of fish, there is guidance on correct portion allowances and a comparison between the nutritional values of oily and white fish. Step-by-step photos make preparation such as scaling, gutting, skinning and filleting simple and understandable. Then there is a graphic description of the most common cooking methods in classical fish cuisine. And just before the main recipes, there is a revealing illustrated section on the correct way to eat fish and seafood.

The book is divided into four main chapters. The first, "Great Hors d'Oeuvres", features the various first courses in which the main ingredient is fish. There are classic but imaginative fish soups, plus snacks and light entrées, as well as classical starters featuring both fish and shellfish. "Exquisite Main Dishes" begins with simple recipes like fillet of plaice, trout au bleu and rolled sole, and then progresses to heartier dishes like waterzooi, a classic Belgian fish dish, dishes using eel in various ways, clam chowder and bouillabaisse. The next chapter, "Special Occasion Dishes", contains classic hot and cold dishes, such as quenelles de brochet (pike dumplings), pike-perch in a salt shell, gilt-poll Roman style, fish pies and mousse. The final chapter, "Party Meals", is intended to provide ideas for entertaining, for instance, a fish fondue, a Russian-style pirog, spinach flan or trout pie. The recipes for barbecued fish provide ideas for informal entertaining, especially the marinated fish and big fish salads. This section is followed by a page of step-by-step photos showing the preparation of fine fish sauces.

The 16 pages of notes on common species and highly-prized or interesting fish and seafood are supplemented with clear and informative illustrations in the section "Recognising Fish and Shellfish". The fish are grouped in their zoological families. Most names are given in French, Italian, Spanish and German to help on visits abroad. The main fishing grounds are listed, along with average sizes, particular habits, the fat content of the species and the condition in which the fish come to market. There is information on whether the fish must be scaled, which methods of preparation are most suitable and how to cook the fish successfully, even in unusual combinations.

Enough about this book. Let the many tempting colour photos inspire you to make more room for fish and seafood in your meal plans.

Wishing you every success and bon appetit
Annette Wolter and colleagues

All recipes serve four, unless stated otherwise.

The abbreviations kJ and kcal in the recipes stand for kilo joules and kilocalories, respectively.

The Value of Fish

It is common knowledge that both freshwater and saltwater fish contain valuable proteins, vitamins and trace elements, the quality and quantities of which few other foods can match. From the nutritional and physiological point of view, fish protein is almost as valuable as that of hen's eggs, but, with the exception of some shellfish, the cholesterol content is much lower. Fish oil contains a large proportion of polyunsaturates which are needed because the human body is unable to synthesise them. The typical flavour of freshwater and sea fish is unique and, unlike meat, remains uncontaminated by whatever the fish itself has eaten. To retain the food value of fish it is necessary to bear one or two points in mind when handling fish and seafood.

The range of fresh fish
There are far more varieties of fish at the fishmongers than those described briefly at the end of this book. When shopping for fish, the most important factor is freshness. Fresh fish can be seriously affected by incorrect storage. So use your eyes and nose to give your chosen fishmonger's an initial check. There should be no overpowering fishy smell; at the most, the shop should smell of the sea and seaweed. Fish must be stored on ice or in chilled cabinets. You can spot fresh fish by their clear, shining, round eyes, their bright pink gills, the smooth, shiny - but not slimy - skin and firm flesh.

Shopping tips
• Only choose the fish for your next meal when you arrive at the fishmonger's.
• Get the fishmonger to prepare the fish for cooking, that is,

cleaned and scaled or filleted as necessary.
• A good fish stock or soup requires trimmings such as heads, fins and tails. Ask the fishmonger for these items, who will often give

you additional trimmings free with your purchase.
• The shells of live shellfish must be tightly shut. Open shells are a sign of dead or dying shellfish, which are inedible.
• When buying live crustaceans, be sure that they are either moving normally in their tank or else struggle vigorously when held out of water.

How large should fish portions be?
For filleted fish, reckon on 200g/7oz per person. In the case of whole fish, make an allowance of up to 50% wastage. Allow at least 300g/10oz per person in the case of small fish and 350-450g/11-16oz per person for large fish cooked whole and divided before serving. For mussels and oysters allow 500g/1lb 2oz and six to twelve per person, respectively. Allow one whole lobster or spiny lobster (langouste) weighing about 700g/1lb 9oz as a main course, or half this amount for a starter. About 250-300g/8-10oz is a fair portion of smaller shellfish in the shell; if shelled, allow 150-200g/5½-7oz.

Preparing fresh fish
For best results, buy fish fresh on the day you intend to use it. Remove the fish from its wrapping and place in a covered china bowl in the refrigerator until the time comes to prepare it. Only in exceptional circumstances should fish be kept for 24 hours in these conditions.

Frozen fish
Frozen fish and seafood usually come ready to cook, and therefore produce no waste. For the most part, sea fish are filleted and frozen on factory ships; large fish are sawn into blocks, small fish are filleted or frozen whole and packed. "Frozen at sea" is the indication to look for on the packaging. Shellfish and crustaceans are killed by boiling and are immediately frozen either in the shell or pre-prepared. Freshwater fish are processed as appropriate by frozen food producers. The quality of frozen fish and seafood is excellent, provided it is treated as directed on the packet. Shellfish and crustaceans are best left to thaw slowly, unpacked but covered, in a refrigerator. Fillets need only light defrosting. Large steaks or whole fish should be unpacked and left covered in a refrigerator to thaw thoroughly (8 to 12 hours).

Beware of unlabelled deep-frozen items
Avoid buying frozen fish without its packaging or in packaging without a manufacturer's name. Fishmongers may sell fish that is frozen on the premises and subsequently thawed. This must be consumed on the same day, without fail.

Nutritional value of fish
The distinction between white and oily fish is quite loose because some fish are neither one nor the other. However, this abbreviated guide gives approximate kilojoule (kJ) and kilocalorie (kCal) values, as well as protein, fat and carbohydrate contents. For 100g/4oz of flesh, oily species like eels, herrings and mackerel provide 525-1170kJ/125-280kCal, 15-20g protein, 6-25g fat, 0g carbohydrate. For a similar quantity, white fish like trout, cod, haddock, sole and pike-perch provide 295-500kJ/70-120kcal, 17-20g protein, 0.1-5g fat and 0g carbohydrate.

Preparing Fish Correctly

Scaling

Most fish must be scaled before cooking. However, a recent technique is to poach, steam and grill fish with the scales on, to conserve the flavour, and to leave the scaly skin untouched when eating the fish. When preparing dishes containing unscaled fish in sauce, pass the sauce through a sieve to avoid scales finding their way into the sauce.

When scaling the fish, first remove dorsal, ventral and lateral fins with scissors. At this stage, depending on the recipe and type of fish, remove the head with a sharp knife.

Cleaning

This is often unnecessary because fish are generally displayed ready to cook; otherwise the fishmonger will clean the fish when it is sold. However, anyone who cooks their own catch, buys freshly caught fish from an angler or trawlerman will need to know how to clean it.

Where appropriate, scale the fish before cleaning. Then take a sharp knife, slit the belly of the fish open from tail to head and carefully remove the viscera, without damaging the gall bladder.

Skinning

Gourmet recipes involving flatfish sometimes call for the fish to be skinned; this must also be done before filleting. However, when cutting large flat fish into pieces for poaching, the skin should be left on even though it is not eaten. Sole and halibut are rarely skinned. When preparing whole flat fish, turbot for instance, the top skin is removed; in the case of flounders, the dark skin is stripped off and discarded.

For all flat fish, except lemon sole, make an angled cut in the skin near the tail and loosen it until there is enough to grip. Then hold both tail and skin with a cloth or kitchen paper and pull the skin smoothly and firmly towards the head.

Filleting Round Fish

This is slightly more difficult than filleting flat fish. Flat fish yield four fillets whereas round fish divide into only two which are thicker and longer and not so easily removed.

First make a cut to the depth of the backbone from head to tail, using a sharp knife. Then insert the knife through the fish from the back to the belly, just below the gills, and lift the flesh slightly.

Wrap the tail of the fish in a cloth and hold it firmly. Using the back of a knife, scrape the fish from tail to head, 'against the grain', under running water into a sink to prevent the scales from flying in all directions.

Do not scale fish that are to be prepared 'au bleu' as this destroys the layer over the skin that gives the fish its colour. Simply wash the fish inside and out under running water; do not rub or dry the fish.

Remove the liver from the entrails, wash it, and use it in a sauce or fry it. Rub the inside of the fish with salt to remove any remaining membranes and traces of blood, then rinse under cold water.

Wash the cleaned fish, including the head, thoroughly under cold water. If large fish are to be cooked whole, make four diagonal slits from the belly to the backbone to assist even cooking of thick and thin sections, and to reduce cooking time.

When skinning lemon sole, make a cut in the skin below the gills and loosen it until there is enough to grip. Then hold both head and skin with a cloth or kitchen paper and pull the skin towards the tail.

If the skinned fish is to be filleted, divide the fillets along the backbone. Using a sharp knife, make small cuts along the ribs towards the outside of each fillet while pulling outwards with your other hand.

Make small cuts with the point of a knife, working towards the belly and releasing the flesh from the backbone. Turn the fish over and repeat the process on the other side.

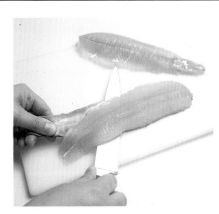

Place the fillets skin side down on a board. Starting at the tail end, carefully draw your knife along between the skin and the fillet to remove the skin. Keep the skin gripped firmly with your other hand.

Cooking Methods

Fish au Bleu

Freshwater fish such as eel, trout, pike, carp, char and tench whose skin is covered with a layer of mucous can be prepared 'au bleu'. Do not scale the fish, just wash it, without removing the layer which causes the blue colouration.

To make a fish court-bouillon, cut one large onion into rings and slice one carrot, then simmer them in about 2 l/3¹/₂ pints of water for 20 minutes, with three parsley sprigs and 1 tsp of salt. Then add a bay leaf, six allspice grains and six white peppercorns and simmer for a further 10 minutes.

Poaching

This is cooking by immersion in hot liquid, just below boiling point. Depending on the desired result, use the same court-bouillon as for cooking 'au bleu' above, but use lemon juice as a substitute for vinegar. The bouillon mixed with wine is later used to prepare a sauce, combined with cream or crème fraîche if desired.

Thoroughly wash about 600g/1lb 6oz of fish trimmings such as heads, fins and tails. Cover them in water and boil for about 30 minutes with one finely chopped onion, two parsley sprigs, 50g/2oz of sliced mushrooms, half a bay leaf, six white peppercorns and a thyme sprig. Skim as necessary.

Braising

This method is particularly good at conserving the goodness of fillets or steaks because the fish juices blend with the small amounts of other juices, forming the basis for a fine aromatic sauce.

Dice one or two shallots, cut a carrot into strips and thinly slice a stick of celery. Fry the vegetables in 15-25g/¹/₂-1oz butter. Add 125ml/4fl oz of dry white wine, fish stock or weak poultry stock and bring to the boil.

Steaming

For steaming large fish, use a fish kettle with a basket; for smaller fish or steaks use a pan large enough to accommodate a flameproof plate standing on a pair of flameproof ramekins.

Lightly butter the basket and place the fish in it. Fill the kettle to a depth of about 2cm/³/₄ inch with a mixture of half fish stock and half white wine and bring to the boil. Place the fish over the stock and steam it in the tightly covered kettle for 10-15 minutes, depending on the size of fish.

Pour the court-bouillon into a fish kettle or large pan, add 250ml/9fl oz of white wine vinegar or sherry vinegar and allow the liquid to cool. Place a large fish on the trivit in the fish kettle in the cooled court-bouillon, bring it to a simmer and cook the fish for 15-20 minutes.

When cooking smaller fish, place them into a simmering court-bouillon and regulate the heat so that the surface bubbles only occasionally. Keep some cold water at hand to allow you to make rapid alterations to the temperature. The fish must be covered with court-bouillon at all times; depending on weight, it will need 7-10 minutes cooking.

Sieve the court-bouillon and transfer it to a fish kettle, adding 500ml/16fl oz of dry white wine. Place a large fish on the fish kettle trivit and lower it into the cooled court-bouillon. Heat the court-bouillon until it is just below its boiling point and leave the fish for 5 minutes over a very low heat. Remove the fish kettle from the stove and leave it to stand for a further 10 minutes.

When cooking smaller fish, place them directly into the heated court-bouillon, which should be just below its boiling point. Leave for 5 minutes on the stove, then for a further 3-5 minutes in the liquid without further addition of heat. The fish are cooked when the eyes take on a whitish appearance, the remains of the dorsal fin can be easily removed, the flesh is light in colour and no traces of blood can be seen.

Place the fish on the vegetables, salt them lightly and cover the pan tightly. Cook over a low heat for 10-15 minutes, depending on the size and weight of the fish. If necessary add a little extra liquid (water or stock).

Place the fish on a heated plate over a layer of vegetables and keep hot. Add some more water, wine or stock to the steaming juices if desired, stir in some cream or crème fraîche, cook for a while, season and pour it over the fish.

Place small fish, fillets or steaks on a flameproof plate. In a pan of an appropriate size, bring a mixture of half fish stock, half white wine, to the boil and stand two flameproof ramekins in this stock. Place the plate on top of these and steam the fish in the tightly covered pan for 7-10 minutes, depending on the size of fish.

The juice that collects on the plate during steaming, can be used instead of a sauce. The court-bouillon in the fish kettle can also be used to pour over the fish.

Cooking Methods

Baking

Large whole fish, fish steaks or fillets may be baked. The best way is to use foil because the protective wrapping prevents the fish from drying out, and the juices do not evaporate, but thanks to the special properties of foil, the fish will still brown.

Place the prepared fish in the foil with finely-shredded vegetables, herbs and a little liquid such as fish stock, wine, milk or poultry stock. Sour cream, crème fraîche, double cream or thick-set natural yogurt may be added at this stage.

Frying

Small fish weighing up to about 250g/8oz, fish steaks and fillets can be pan-fried. The short cooking time in hot oil means that the fish does not dry out and the crisp layer that forms gives a pleasant aroma.

Pat the fish dry. Salt and season the fish steaks or fillets, and the insides of whole fish. For each fish mix together about a tablespoon of flour with a little salt and freshly ground white pepper.

Grilling

Cooking on an electric or gas grill is easier than over charcoal. Intense heat can easily dry fish out. For this reason, fish should only be charcoal-grilled if the grill has some height adjustment that will allow the fish to be kept at the right distance from the glowing coals.

Oily fish are good for grilling. Other types should be brushed with seasoned oil once or twice during cooking. Turn fish regularly. Cover with greaseproof paper if they are browning too quickly.

Deep Frying

Deep-frying in hot oil is a good method for cooking small fish, fillets, fish cut into strips, prawns and mussels. They may be lightly-floured before frying or breaded. Delicate fish, prawns and mussels are best protected from the intense heat of deep-frying by a batter.

Mix about 2 tsps of lemon juice with 2 tbsps of olive oil and a pinch of freshly ground white pepper. Toss the prepared fish, scallops or prawns in this mixture, cover and marinate for 1-2 hours in the refrigerator.

Close the foil package well and use a needle to make about ten holes in the top. Place the fish directly on the shelf second from the bottom of an oven heated to 200°C/400°F/Gas Mark 6. Bake for 10-20 minutes, depending on the size of fish.

Cut the foil package open along the top. Use a roasting fork and slotted spoon to place the fish on a heated dish and pour the juice from the foil with the vegetables, or through a sieve, over the fish.

Carefully turn the fish or pieces in the seasoned flour; they should be lightly but evenly coated. Gently shake to remove any excess flour. If desired, fillets can be dipped in lightly-beaten egg yolk after the flour, and then in a dish of dry breadcrumbs, before frying.

Heat some clarified butter, oil or other cooking fat and fry the fish on both sides over a medium heat for about 1 minute. Turn the heat down and, depending on their size, continue to fry the steaks, fillets or fish for a further 3-7 minutes, turning occasionally.

When grilling over charcoal, fish should be wrapped in oiled aluminium foil. If you want the pattern of the grill to appear on the skin of the fish, place the fish directly on the wire rack for about 1 minute each side, just before cooking is complete.

A heavy-based frying-pan is also perfect for cooking oily fish. Lightly oil the pan, heat well and place the fish in the pan for 4-10 minutes each side, depending on their size. Turn the heat down well once the pan has heated through.

For the batter, mix 150g/5¹/₂oz with 2 egg yolks and enough dry white wine (or beer if desired) to make a smooth batter. Allow it to rest for 30 minutes. Heat the oil in the deep-fryer to 180°C/350°F. Beat 2-3 egg whites with a pinch of salt until stiff and fold into the batter.

Dip the fish, prawns or mussels in the batter, allow them to drain a little, then fry them for 1-5 minutes, depending on their size. Turn larger pieces during frying. Drain them on absorbent kitchen paper. A cold mayonnaise sauce is perfect with deep-fried fish.

13

How to Eat Fish and Seafood

Fish 'Au Bleu'

Fish served 'au bleu', such as trout or carp, are not scaled, and the diner should leave the skin on the plate. The cooked coating of fish tossed in flour or batter, however, has a delicious flavour.

1 Halve the upper fillet along its length, loosen it from the backbone and lift the fillet piece-by-piece with a fish knife.

2 Once the upper half has been eaten, the whole of the backbone, complete with the head, is removed from the lower fillet, starting at the tail.

3 Before the skeleton of a trout becomes cold, a connoisseur will remove the cheeks from beneath the eyes; they are especially delicious.

4 Using a fish knife and fork, the two lower fillets are now peeled away from the skin and eaten.

Mussels

Even inland, mussels are a common dish. Other types of shellfish, including scallops and clams, can be served in the same way.

1 Cooked in a seasoned wine bouillon, with the aroma of finely chopped vegetables, mussels are among the most popular of hors d'oeuvre.

2 They are served in soup plates with a small amount of the cooking liquid. In the case of bivalves, a whole, empty shell can used like a pair of tweezers to scoop out the flesh.

3 It is perfectly acceptable to use your fingers, the natural tool, to extract cooked mussels from their open shells.

4 Any remaining flesh that has already come loose from the shells is eaten with a soup spoon, along with the delicious cooking liquid.

It is a long time since there were strict rules or 'only one correct' way to eat fish, swallow an oyster, or peel a prawn. But one likes to feel comfortable at the table and enjoy the delicacies of sea and stream without embarrassment. Anyone who is not quite sure how to go about it will perhaps find some welcome pointers in these step-by-step pictures.

Grilled Scampi

Small prawns are not tailed before grilling because the delicate flesh can dry out.

1 They are especially tasty when grilled with plenty of garlic oil or garlic butter. Fresh white French bread should be served as an accompaniment.

2 The dark intestine (usually known as the vein) can be seen on the outside of the curve of the body. This is removed first with the point of a knife.

3 Use a knife and fork to lever the two halves out of the shell.

4 When eating the scampi halves, try and take as much of the savoury grilling oil as possible.

Sole

Sole is among the most popular fish. Lemon sole and witch-sole are reasonably priced, but Dover sole is the most expensive flatfish. Rolled sole is a great delicacy, but a large middle cut of Dover sole is a feast.

1 Sole simply fried and seasoned with just a few finely chopped vegetables is a gourmet dish for a connoisseur.

2 When eating flatfish, the two upper fillets are divided by cutting along the visible line and releasing the fillet from the bone.

3 Once the second fillet has been eaten in the same way, the backbone is removed complete with head and tail from the two lower fillets and laid on a spare plate.

4 The two lower fillets can now be separated from the skin easily and eaten with the sauce or other accompaniment.

Great Hors d'Oeuvres

Delicious soups, piquant morsels
and tempting fish cuisine classics

Exquisite Crayfish Soups

Just right for festive occasions and the most demanding guests

Cold Cream of Crayfish Soup
Illustrated above left

40g/1½oz butter
2 tbsps flour
750ml/24fl oz hot chicken stock
4 tbsps crayfish or shrimp paste
2 tbsps brandy
Pinch of cayenne pepper
200ml/6fl oz double cream
50g/2oz long-grain rice
500ml/16fl oz water
Pinch of salt
120g/5oz canned crayfish flesh
Sprig of dill

Preparation time: 1½ hours
Nutritional value:

Analysis per serving, approx:
• 1465kJ/350kcal
• 15g protein
• 72g fat
• 20g carbohydrate

Melt the butter in a saucepan. Stir in the flour over a low heat until the mixture turns bright yellow. Gradually add the chicken stock. Bring the soup to the boil. Remove the pan from the stove and whisk the crayfish or shrimp paste into the soup. Bring the soup to the boil then add the brandy and cayenne pepper. Pour the soup into a bowl and stir in 4 tbsps of cream. Allow the soup to cool, stirring occasionally with a whisk. • Wash the rice thoroughly. Bring the salted water to the boil, add the rice and simmer over a low heat for 20 minutes. Drain and leave to cool. • Whip the rest of the cream until stiff. Cut the crayfish flesh into pieces if necessary and divide it with the rice between four soup plates. Pour the cold soup over it and decorate each with a tablespoon of whipped cream. Garnish the cream with a washed sprig of dill.

Classic Crayfish Soup
Illustrated above right

40g/1½oz rice
500ml/16fl oz meat stock
16 crayfish, each weighing 80g/3oz
1 small carrot • 2 shallots
80g/3oz butter
½ bay leaf • 1 bunch parsley
Pinch of salt and white pepper
3 tbsps brandy
375ml/14fl oz dry white wine
4 tbsps single cream
Pinch of cayenne pepper

Preparation time: 1½ hours
Nutritional value:

Analysis per serving, approx:
• 1860kJ/445kcal • 27g protein
• 22g fat • 16g carbohydrate

Cook the rice in the stock for 20 minutes until soft. • Place the crayfish one-by-one in boiling salted water, and cook for 5 minutes. Remove them with a slotted spoon. • Chop the carrot and shallots finely and fry in 20g/¾oz butter. Add a further 20g/¾oz butter, the bay leaf, parsley and the crayfish. Sprinkle with the salt and pepper. Cook the crayfish on full heat, sprinkle with the cognac and flambé briefly. Add the wine. Cover and simmer the crayfish for 10 minutes. • Remove the crayfish from their shells. Mince the shells and claws in a food processor and cook this with the wine and vegetable stock. Strain the stock through a fine sieve. Discard the bay leaf and parsley, and purée the rest of the vegetables or press them through the sieve. Return them to the pot with the liquid and simmer for 15 minutes. • Beat in the cream. Season with cayenne pepper. Cut the rest of the butter into small pieces and whisk it into the soup. • Slice the crayfish tails and serve them in the soup.

Gourmet Soups with Scampi and Shrimp

The flavour of summer and holidays in the sun

Cucumber and Dill Soup with Shrimp

Illustrated above left

1 onion
1 clove of garlic
30g/1oz butter
1tsp flour
375ml/14fl oz meat stock
1 cucumber
375ml/14fl oz cream
Pinch each of salt, sugar and white pepper
Pinch of mustard powder
200g/7oz shrimps in their shells
2 bunches of dill

Preparation time: 30 minutes
Nutritional value:
Analysis per serving, approx:
- 960kJ/230kcal
- 11g protein
- 17g fat
- 7g carbohydrate

Chop the onion and garlic finely and fry in 10g/¹⁄₄oz of butter until transparent. Add the flour, fry until bright yellow, then add the stock. Wash the cucumber, trim the top and tail and cut off four think slices. Reserve them. Peel the remaining cucumber, cut it in half along its length, scrape the seeds out with a spoon and chop the flesh into 2cm/³⁄₄-inch cubes. Boil the cucumber cubes in the liquid for 15 minutes. • Purée the soup in a liquidiser. Add the cream. Season well with salt, sugar, pepper and mustard powder and simmer over a gentle heat for 5 minutes. • Peel and de-vein the shrimps. • Heat the remaining butter in a pan and fry the shrimps briefly. Wash and chop the dill, then stir it into the soup. • Pour the soup into heated soup plates and add the shrimps and cucumber slices.

Cream of Scampi Soup with Chives

Illustrated above right

4 small tomatoes
4 shallots
2 tbsps butter
1 tbsp flour
6 tbsps dry white wine
250ml/8fl oz hot chicken stock
400ml/15fl oz single cream
Pinch each of salt and sugar
Pinch of freshly ground white pepper
5 drops Tabasco sauce
250g/8oz freshly peeled scampi
2 bunches chives

Preparation time: 40 minutes
Nutritional value:
Analysis per serving, approx:
- 2130kJ/510kcal
- 15g protein
- 42g fat
- 15g carbohydrate

Wash the tomatoes. cut a cross in each top and bottom, then plunge them briefly into boiling water. Skin them, cut them in half and remove the pips. Cut the flesh into small cubes. Chop the shallots very finely and fry in the butter until transparent. Add the flour and fry, stirring constantly, dilute with the white wine. Stir in the chicken stock and add the cream. Allow the soup to come to the boil briefly, then season it with the salt, sugar, pepper and Tabasco sauce. Leave over a gentle heat for 5 minutes. • Heat the washed prawns and diced tomatoes in the soup. Wash the chives, pat them dry and chop finely; stir about 2 tbsps of chive rings into the soup. • Serve the soup in heated soup plates, sprinkled with the remaining chives.

Chinese Fish Soup

Fish plays an important role in Chinese cooking

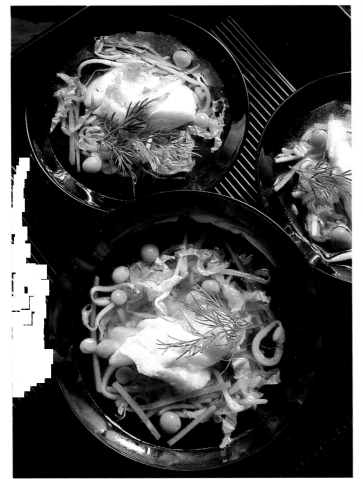

100g/4oz carrots
500g/1lb 2oz Chinese cabbage
2 tbsps sesame oil
100g/4oz brown rice
4 tbsps soy sauce
100g/4oz shelled green peas
200g/7oz canned soya bean sprouts
500g/1lb 2oz cod fillet
2 tbsps lemon juice
3 pinches of five-spice powder
2 tbsps finely chopped fresh dill

Preparation time: 1 hour
Nutritional value:
Analysis per serving, approx:
• 1190kJ/285kcal
• 28g protein
• 6g fat
• 27g carbohydrate

Wash and clean the carrots and Chinese cabbage, then cut them into strips. • Heat the oil in a large pan. Fry the rice for 5 minutes. Add the prepared vegetables and fry for a further 5 minutes. Add 1 l/1¾ pints of hot water and 2 tbsps of soy sauce and simmer for 20 minutes. • Add the peas and soya bean sprouts. • Wash the fish and squeeze the lemon juice over it, then cook it on the bed of vegetables for 10 minutes or until tender. •Remove the fish and break it into pieces with a fork. Remove the pan from the stove. Season the soup with the remaining soy sauce and five-spice powder. Stir in the dill and fish chunks.

Our Tip: Soy sauce is an indispensable ingredient in oriental cookery. Shoyo and Tamari are brands available in health food shops which are both naturally produced and therefore especially aromatic.

Solyanka

This hearty Russian soup can replace a main dish

1 onion
375g/12oz floury potatoes
1 bunch pot herbs (leek, carrot, turnip, swede, etc.)
2 tbsps olive oil
4 tbsps wholewheat flour
1 tsp mushroom ketchup
2 tbsps tomato purée
1 bay leaf
1 l/1¾ pints hot water or meat stock
500g/1lb 2oz redfish or cod fillet
250g/8oz pickled gherkins
250g/8oz beef tomatoes
4 tsps capers
200ml/6fl oz sour cream
1-2 tbsps soy sauce
1-2 tbsps mushroom ketchup
1 tbsp lemon juice
2 tbsps finely chopped fresh dill

Preparation time: 20 minutes
Nutritional value:
Analysis per serving, approx:
• 1525kJ/365kcal
• 29g protein
• 14g fat
• 29g carbohydrate

Dice the onions and potatoes. Wash, clean and chop the pot herbs. • Heat the oil in a large pan. Fry the prepared vegetables. Sprinkle with flour and mushroom ketchup, add the tomato purée and bay leaf and stir. Gradually add the water or stock, bring to the boil and stir until smooth. • Wash the fish and add to the soup. Cook for 10 minutes over gentle heat until tender. • Dice the gherkins and cut the washed tomatoes into eighths • Break the fish into chunks and divide it between four heated plates. Add the capers, gherkins and tomatoes to the soup and allow them to cook for about a minute. Remove the pan from the heat. Beat the sour cream with the soy sauce and lemon juice and stir into the soup. • Serve the Solyanka with a sprinkling of fresh dill.

Clear Soups with Fish Dumplings

These soups are appetising, light and digestible

Vegetable Soup with Smoked Salmon Dumplings

Illustrated above left

50g/2oz millet
125ml/4fl oz milk
100g/4oz smoked salmon
½ small onion
1 bunch of parsley
1 egg
3 tbsps wholewheat flour
Pinch of ground cumin
1 bunch of pot herbs (leek, carrot, turnip, swede, etc.)
1 l/1¾ pints water
3 tsps vegetable stock granules
250g/8oz cauliflower florets
150g/5 ½oz shelled green peas

Preparation time: 1 hour
Nutritional value:
- 670kJ/160kcal
- 10g protein
- 3g fat
- 22g carbohydrate

Sift the millet, then pour it into 125ml/4 fl oz boiling water. Cook for 15 minutes over a gentle heat. • Add the milk and simmer for 5 minutes. Remove the pan from the heat. Cover it and allow the millet to swell in the liquid for 5 minutes; drain through a sieve. • Chop the salmon and onion coarsely, mince in a food processor with 2 sprigs of parsley and the millet, then blend together with the egg, flour and cumin. • Wash, trim and chop the potherbs and bring the water to the boil in a saucepan. Add the potherbs and stock granules. Wash the cauliflower and peas and add them to the pan. Use two spoons to form the dough into dumplings. Slip the dumplings into the soup, cover the pan and simmer for 15 minutes over a gentle heat. • Finely chop the remaining parsley and stir it into the soup.

Dill Soup with Fish Dumplings

Illustrated above right

200g/7oz coley fillet
1 onion
100g/4oz wholewheat flour
1 tsp sea salt
3 eggs
2 tbsps lemon juice
2 tbsps finely chopped fresh dill
Pinch of freshly ground white pepper
4 tsps dill seeds
1 bunch pot herbs (leek, carrot, turnip, swede, etc.)
1½ l/2¼ pints water
1 tbsp finely chopped fresh parsley
2 tsps garlic salt

Preparation time: 1 hour
Nutritional value:
Analysis per serving, approx:
- 1650kJ/395kcal
- 20g protein
- 2g fat
- 70g carbohydrate

Wash the fish and chop it coarsely. Chop the onion into quarters. To make the dumplings, mince the fish and onion very finely in a food processor, then mix with the flour, salt, eggs, 1 tbsp lemon juice, 1 tbsp dill and the pepper. • Roast the dill seeds in a dry frying-pan over a gentle heat for 2 or 3 minutes. Wash and clean the pot herbs, then cut them into fine strips and cook them with the dill seeds in boiling water for 10 minutes. With wet hands, form the dumpling mixture into small balls and slip them into the boiling liquid. Cover, and cook the dumplings over a gentle heat for 10 minutes. • Remove the pan from the heat. Sprinkle the soup with the remaining dill and the parsley, garlic salt and lemon juice, and season with white pepper if necessary.

Cream of Salmon Soup

An unusual gourmet soup

375g/6 oz fresh salmon trimmings
1 onion
1 bay leaf
Pinch of salt
500ml/16fl oz water
Few white peppercorns
500g/1lb 2oz fresh salmon
25g/1oz butter
1tbsp flour
125ml/4fl oz cream
125ml/4fl oz crème fraîche
Pinch each of freshly ground white pepper and powdered saffron
½ tsp lemon juice
100g/4oz smoked salmon
Few chervil sprigs

Preparation time: 20 minutes
Cooking time: 45 minutes
Nutritional value:
Analysis per serving, approx:
• 2340kJ/560kcal
• 32g protein
• 45g fat
• 5g carbohydrate

Rinse the salmon trimmings under cold water. Chop the onion into quarters and poach them in water for 30 minutes with the salmon trimmings, the bay leaf, salt and peppercorns. • Strain the stock into a saucepan. Wash the salmon, place it in the stock and simmer for 12-15 minutes over a gentle heat. • Remove the skin and bones from the fish and flake the flesh. • Measure out 375ml/14 fl oz of stock and strain through a sieve. • Heat the butter in a pan. Stir in the flour, then gradually add the fish stock. Add the cream and crème fraîche. Season with salt, pepper, saffron and lemon juice. Bring the soup to the boil, then remove it from the heat. • Place the salmon in the soup. Cut the smoked salmon into strips. • Serve the soup in heated plates; garnish with the smoked salmon strips and the chervil.

Fish Soup with Potatoes

The mixture of freshwater fish in this Finnish soup makes it rather unusual

750g/1lb10oz freshwater fish, such as perch, trout or tench
500g/1lb 2oz potatoes
1 large onion or 1 leek
8 grains allspice
1 bay leaf
½ tbsp salt
25g/1oz butter
100ml/3fl oz sour cream
Pinch of white pepper
1 bunch dill

Preparation time: 30 minutes
Cooking time: 35 minutes
Nutritional value:
Analysis per serving, approx:
• 1570kJ/375kcal
• 40g protein
• 13g fat
• 23g carbohydrate

Clean the fish and wash it thoroughly under running water. Dab it dry and cut it into large pieces. Peel, wash and dice the potatoes, but not too finely. Cut the onion into rings, or wash and clean the leek, then cut into rings. • Place the potato, onion or leek rings, allspice and bay leaf in a casserole or pot from which the finished soup can be served. Add the fish pieces. Sprinkle the fish with salt, then chop the butter into pieces and scatter it over the ingredients. Add water to cover and simmer for 35 minutes. • Stir the sour cream into the soup and season with salt and pepper. Wash the dill, dry it and chop it finely. Sprinkle over the soup just before serving. • Rye crispbread makes a delicious accompaniment.

Barley Soup with Fish

Fish in an unusual combination

| 100g/4oz pearl barley |
| 1 l/1³/₄ pints water |
| 1 bay leaf |
| 1 tbsp vegetable stock granules |
| 1 bunch pot herbs |
| 400g/14oz coley fillet |
| 100g/4oz shelled green peas |
| Pinch each of dried thyme, marjoram and basil |
| 100g/4oz smoked mackerel fillet |
| 100g/4oz shrimps |
| 2 tbsps finely chopped fresh parsley |
| 3 pinches freshly ground black pepper |
| 2-3 tbsps lemon juice |

Soaking time: 12 hours
Preparation time: 35 minutes
Nutritional value:
Analysis per serving, approx:
• 1110kJ/265kcal
• 31g protein
• 5g fat
• 21g carbohydrate

Soak the barley in water for 12 hours or overnight. • Rinse, drain and add to a pot with the water, bay leaf and stock granules. Boil for 15 minutes. • Wash, clean and chop the pot herbs. Wash the coley fillet and add it to the liquid, together with the pot herbs, peas and dried herbs. Simmer for a further 15 minutes. • Check the mackerel fillet for any remaining, stray bones and discard them. Remove the coley and break it and the smoked mackerel into pieces. De-vein the shrimps and rinse them. Stir them into the soup with the fish pieces and parsley; season with pepper, lemon juice and a few extra stock granules if necessary.

Cream of Fish Soup

The mixed vegetables make this an interesting soup

| 100g/4oz each leeks, carrots and mushrooms |
| 300g/10oz courgettes |
| 3 tbsps sesame oil |
| 1 l/1³/₄ pints hot water |
| 1 tbsp vegetable stock granules |
| 400g/14oz cod fillet |
| 3 tbsps lemon juice |
| 4 tbsps wholemeal flour |
| 100ml/3fl oz cream |
| 2 tbsps tomato purée |
| 2 pinches freshly ground white pepper |
| 1-2 tsps garlic salt |
| 2 dill sprigs |

Preparation time: 35 minutes
Nutritional value:
Analysis per serving, approx:
• 1255kJ/300kcal
• 21g protein
• 16g fat
• 16g carbohydrate

Wash, clean and thinly slice the vegetables. Heat the oil in a large frying-pan and fry the vegetables for about 5 minutes, stirring constantly. Add the water and stock granules and bring to the boil. Wash the fish and sprinkle with 2 tbsps lemon juice, and arrange it on the bed of vegetables in the pan. Cook for 15 minutes over a gentle heat. • Blend the vegetables with the liquid and 200g/7oz fish in a food processor, return to the pan and bring to the boil. Mix the flour with the cream and tomato purée. Stir this mixture into the soup and cook for 2 or 3 minutes. • Break the remaining fish into small pieces and heat in the soup. Remove the pan from the heat and season the soup with pepper, garlic salt and the remaining lemon juice; garnish with dill sprigs.

Pea Soup with Shrimps

High in protein, packed with vitamins and so tasty!

1 onion
25g/1oz butter
400g/14oz shelled green peas
750ml/1¼ pints hot meat stock
250g/8oz shrimps
125ml/4fl oz dry white wine
Pinch of freshly ground pepper
2 pinches dried basil
Pinch of sugar
125ml/4fl oz sour cream
2 egg yolks

Preparation time: 30 minutes
Nutritional value:
Analysis per serving, approx:
• 1255kJ/300kcal
• 20g protein
• 14g fat
• 18g carbohydrate

Chop the onion finely. Heat the butter in a frying-pan and fry the onion until it turns transparent. Add the peas and cover with the meat stock. Heat the liquid gently for 10 minutes. • Heat the oven to 240°C/450°F/Gas Mark 8. • De-vein the shrimps. Rinse and drain the shrimps. Mix the soup with the white wine and season with pepper, basil and sugar. Put the shrimps in the soup to heat, but do not bring to the boil. Beat the sour cream with the egg yolks. Divide the soup between four flameproof soup bowls, pour the cream over the surface of the soup, and brown on the top shelf of the oven or under a grill until the layer of cream just begins to colour. • Serve immediately.

Our Tip: When buying fresh peas in their shells, at least half the weight must be allowed as waste. Shelled frozen peas are a substitute of very similar quality.

Cream of Mussel Soup

Try this without fail when fresh mussels are obtainable

1kg/2¼lbs mussels
250ml/8 fl oz dry white wine
50g/2oz streaky bacon • 2 onions
2 tomatoes • 1 carrot
75g/3oz root vegetable (turnip, parsnip, etc.) • 2 tbsps flour
45g/1½ oz butter
125ml/4fl oz cream • 1 egg yolk
Pinch of salt and white pepper

Preparation time: 40 minutes
Cooking time: 30 minutes
Nutritional value:
Analysis per serving, approx:
• 2445kJ/585kcal • 33g protein
• 36g fat • 19g carbohydrate

Wash the mussels thoroughly under cold running water (discard any open shells), place in a large saucepan and pour the white wine over them. Cook until all the shells have opened (discard any that remain closed), shaking the pan from time to time. • Extract the flesh from the shells.

Chop the bacon finely and cut the onion into rings. Make a cross-shaped cut in the tomato skins top and bottom and plunge them in boiling water; skin them, and remove the hard part where the stalk joins the fruit. Chop them into quarters and finally, cubes. Scrape the carrot and slice it into thin strips. Fry the chopped bacon until the fat runs, then add all the vegetables except the carrot and cook them in the bacon fat. Strain the mussel stock and add enough water to make the liquid up to 1l/1¾ pints. Add the liquid to the vegetables and simmer the soup over a gentle heat for 20 minutes. • Strain the soup. Melt the butter, stir in the flour and cook for 2 minutes. Gradually add the vegetable liquid and bring to the boil. Transfer the mussel flesh and carrot strips to the soup pot. • Beat the cream with the egg yolk and mix in 2 tbsps of the hot soup. Use this to thicken and season the soup as desired.

Classic Fish Soups

These soups demonstrate the versatility of fish cookery

Spanish Fish Soup
Illustrated above left

500g/1lb 2oz tomatoes
500g/1lb 2oz red and green peppers
3 onions
3 cloves garlic
6 tbsps olive oil
100g/4oz brown rice
1 1/1¾ pints hot water
500g/1lb 2oz fish fillet, such as redfish, coley or hake
1 tbsp lemon juice
1 tsp finely chopped fresh or ¹/₂ tsp dried rosemary
1 tbsp each of chopped chive and fresh chopped parsley
1 tsp sea salt

Preparation time: 20 minutes
Cooking time: 30 minutes
Nutritional value:
Analysis per serving, approx:
• 1860kJ/445kcal
• 28g protein
• 20g fat
• 34g carbohydrate

Cut a cross in the tomato skins top and bottom, plunge into boiling water, skin and cut into eighths. Quarter and wash the peppers, discarding the seeds and stalk, and slice into thin strips crossways. Finely chop the onions and garlic and fry in the oil until transparent. Add the rice, pepper strips and tomato pieces and quickly fry over high heat for 5 minutes. Add the water. Simmer the soup for 25 minutes. • Wash the fish and sprinkle with lemon juice, divide it into portions and add it to the soup together with the rosemary. Cook for 5 minutes over a gentle heat. • Add the herbs and season with salt.

French Fish Consommé
Illustrated above right

1 bunch of pot herbs (turnip, carrot, leek, celery
1¹/₂l/2¹/₄ pints water
1 bay leaf
5 white peppercorns
2 grains allspice
1 tsp dill seed
250g/8oz beefsteak tomatoes
2 celery stalks
100g/4oz carrots
100g/4oz shelled green peas
400g/14oz white fish fillets (hake, coley or cod)
3-4 tbsps lemon juice
2-3 tsps garlic salt
Few dill sprigs

Preparation time: 30 minutes
Nutritional value:
Analysis per serving, approx:
• 500 kJ/120 kcal • 19g protein
• 0.4g fat • 9g carbohydrate

Wash and clean the pot herbs, chop them coarsely and cook them in water for 15 minutes with the bay leaf, allspice and dill seeds. • Meanwhile, cut a cross in the tomato skins top and bottom, plunge them into boiling water, skin and then dice. Wash the celery and carrots and cut them into thin strips. • Strain the vegetable stock then return it to the boil. Add celery, carrots and the peas. Wash the fish, sprinkle with 1 tbsp of lemon juice and add to the liquid. Cook over a low heat for about 10 minutes until the fish is tender. • Break the fish into pieces and add it to the soup with the diced tomatoes. Season with the remaining lemon juice and garlic salt. Garnish with dill. • A good accompaniment to this dish is wholemeal croûtons, made by rubbing triangles of wholewheat bread with half a clove of garlic, then toasting them.

Maatjes Herrings with Mustard

This is a classic Danish Dish

1 onion, cut into rings
500ml/16fl oz water
125ml/4fl oz vinegar
2 tbsps sugar
4 juniper berries
8 maatjes herring fillets weighing 50g/2oz each
1 untreated orange
125ml/4fl oz cream
1 shallot
2 tsps medium-hot prepared mustard
1 tsp mustard powder

Preparation time: 40 minutes
Marinating time: 1 day
Nutritional value:

Analysis per serving, approx:
• 1820kJ/435kcal
• 18g protein
• 33g fat
• 17g carbohydrate

Boil the water with the vinegar, sugar, juniper berries and onions cut into rings, then allow it to stand and cool. • Cut the maatjes herring fillets into pieces, pour the marinade over them and store them, covered, in a cool place for 24 hours. • Drain off the marinade. Wash the orange and finely shred a small piece of the peel. Remove the rest of the peel and the pith. Slice the orange, then cut the slices into quarters. • Mix the pieces of herring with the onion rings and orange slices. Sprinkle with 1 tsp of shredded orange peel. • Whip the cream until stiff. Peel and finely grate the shallots. Combine the shallots and mustard with the cream. Serve the mustard sauce with the herring.

Canapés with Mackerel Cream

Delicate morsels that go well with an apéritif

Makes 8 canapés:
1 smoked mackerel (about 300g/10oz)
250g/8oz quark
1 tbsp lemon juice
Pinch each of salt, freshly ground white pepper and paprika
4 slices of bread
1¹/₂oz/30g softened butter
4 black olives
15g/¹/₂oz fresh dill

Preparation time: 20 minutes
Nutritional value:

Analysis per serving, approx:
• 880kJ/210kcal
• 13g protein
• 15g fat
• 7g carbohydrate

Separate the mackerel flesh from skin and bones. Purée the fillets, and combine with the quark and lemon juice. Season the cream with salt, pepper and paprika. • Remove crusts from the bread and spread with butter. Cut each slice in half diagonally to produce eight triangles. • Take a piping bag with a large star-shaped nozzle and pipe the mackerel spread over the bread. Stone the olives and cut them into fine strips. Wash the dill and pat dry. Garnish the canapés with strips of olive and dill.

Our Tip: The cream spread ingredients can be varied at will. It tastes marvellous if prepared with 300g/10oz of smoked salmon, for example. In this case, use whipped cream and quark in equal measure. A little lemon juice gives extra zing, and instead of olives, use paper-thin onion rings and strips of smoked salmon as a garnish.

Popular Hors d'Oeuvres Quickly Prepared

Ideal for entertaining

Maatjes Herring Cocktail

Illustrated top

4 maatjes herring fillets
150g/5 ¹/₂oz cooked celery
1 sharp apple • Juice of 1 lemon
2 hard-boiled eggs
2 tbsps wine vinegar
¹/₂ tbsp hot mustard • 1 tbsp oil
1 finely chopped onion
1 tbsp tomato ketchup
Few drops of Tabasco sauce
Salt and pepper

Preparation time: 30 minutes
Nutritional value:
Analysis per serving, approx:
• 940kJ/210kcal • 12g protein
• 14g fat • 11g carbohydrate

Soak the fillets in water for 20 minutes, pat them dry and then dice them with the celery and the peeled apple. Sprinkle with the lemon juice. Mix the egg yolks with the other ingredients. • Coat the cocktail with the sauce and decorate with strips of egg white.

Stuffed Salmon Rolls

Illustrated bottom

1 small sharp apple
1 hard-boiled egg
40g/1¹/₄oz fresh horseradish
1 tbsp lemon juice • 1 tbsp oil
5 tbsp single cream
Pinch each of salt and sugar
8 slices smoked salmon
Few oakleaf lettuce leaves
1 untreated lemon
1-2 dill sprigs

Preparation time: 20 minutes
Nutritional value:
Analysis per serving, approx:
• 1085kJ/260kcal • 20g protein
• 16g fat • 8g carbohydrate

Dice the egg, the peeled apple and horseradish, then blend them in a liquidiser with the oil and cream. Season the resulting purée and spread it on the salmon slices. Roll them up and arrange on lettuce leaves with lemon slices and dill.

Special Fish Snacks

Light snacks, prepared and served in unusual ways

Fish on Cress

Illustrated above left

| 300g/10oz cod fillet |
| 2 tsps tea leaves |
| 2 tbsps lemon juice |
| Pepper • 2 punnets cress |
| 150g/5¹/₂oz low-fat soft cheese |
| 3 tbsps thick-set natural yogurt |
| 1 tbsp tomato purée |
| 1 tbsp apple purée |
| 2 tsps finely chopped capers |
| 2 tsps finely chopped dill |
| ¹/₂ tsp paprika • 1 tsp garlic salt |

Preparation time: 20 minutes
Nutritional value:
Analysis per serving, approx:
• 545kJ/130kcal • 18g protein
• 3g fat • 7g carbohydrate

Wash the cod fillet. Brew the tea in 125ml/4 fl oz boiling water in the steamer pan. Butter the steamer itself and place the fish in it, sprinkle the fish with lemon juice and pepper, and steam for about 10 minutes or until tender. • Divide the cress between four plates. • Make a sauce by combining the quark, cream, tomato and apple purée, 2 tbsps of tea, the capers, dill and paprika. • Arrange the fish on the bed of cress and coat the fish with the sauce. Season with lemon juice and garlic salt.

Fish Crackers

Illustrated above in background

To make 15 crackers:

| 100g/4oz each of buckwheat flour and wholewheat flour |
| 1 tsp baking powder |
| 1 tsp ground caraway seed |
| ¹/₂ tsp salt |
| 100g/4oz margarine |
| 100ml/4fl oz sour cream |
| 200g/7oz soused herring or salted herring fillets, soaked overnight |
| 2 shallots • 3 hard-boiled eggs |
| 200g/7oz crème fraîche |
| 1 tbsp finely chopped dill |

Preparation time: 40 minutes
Baking time: 15 minutes
Nutritional values per cracker:
Analysis per serving, approx:
• 1005kJ/240kcal • 5.5g protein
• 25g fat • 3.5g carbohydrate

Knead the flour, caraway, baking powder, salt, margarine and sour cream into a dough and form a roll about 7cm/2¹/₂in in diameter. Place the roll of dough in the freezer for 30 minutes. • Heat the oven to 200°C/400°F/Gas Mark 6. Slice the dough into 5mm/¹/₄ -inch slices and bake for 15 minutes on a greased baking sheet. Leave on wire racks to cool • Finely chop the herring fillets, shallots and eggs, mix with the crème fraîche and dill; spread on the cooled crackers.

Bloater Toasts

Illustrated above foreground

| 4 slices wholewheat bread |
| 50g/2oz butter • 4 eggs |
| 2 tbsps wholewheat flour |
| 125ml/4fl oz milk |
| 100g/4oz bloater fillets |
| Sea salt • 4 tbsps chopped chives |
| 1 tomato, quartered |

Preparation time: 15 minutes
Nutritional value:
Analysis per serving, approx:
• 960kJ/230kcal • 9g protein
• 13g fat • 17g carbohydrate

Toast the bread and spread it with some of the butter. • Beat the eggs together with the flour and milk. Break the fish into bite-size pieces and fry the pieces briefly in the rest of the butter. Pour the egg mixture over this and allow it to become firm. Stir in the chives and salt. Spread the mixture on the toast and garnish.

Plaice Rolls in Green Peppers

An attractive way of serving rolled plaice

Shrimp Omelettes

A traditional hors d'oeuvre

2 green peppers	
Pinch of salt	
8 plaice fillets	
Juice of 1 lemon	
½ tsp of salt and white pepper	
2 tsps mustard	
1 carrot	
1 bunch parsley	
200g/7oz shrimps in their shells	
250ml/8fl oz cream	
1 egg yolk	
2 tbsps finely chopped fresh dill	

Preparation time: 1 hour
Nutritional value:
Analysis per serving, approx:
• 1570kJ/375kcal • 30g protein
• 23g fat • 10g carbohydrate

Wash the peppers, halve them and discard the seeds. Do not remove the stalks. Blanch the pepper halves in 250ml/9 fl oz of boiling salted water for 3 minutes, then place them in an oven to keep warm. Retain the blanching liquid. • Wash the plaice fillets and pat them dry. Sprinkle them with lemon juice, salt and pepper and spread them with mustard. Roll up the fillets and fasten them with wooden cocktail sticks. Scrape and chop the the carrot and place it in the blanching liquid with the rolled plaice. Add the parsley and cook over a low heat for 6 minutes. • Place 2 rolls in each pepper half and keep warm. • Wash and peel the shrimps and boil the shrimp shells in the fish and vegetable liquid for 15 minutes. • De-vein the shrimps. • Strain the liquid through a fine sieve and reduce to 125ml/4 fl oz. In a separate pan, reduce the cream by half by boiling over high heat, then stir it into the stock. Beat the egg yolk and use it to bind the sauce; season with a little lemon juice. Add the shrimps and allow them to steep for 2 minutes. • Pour the shrimp sauce over the plaice rolls. Serve garnished with the chopped dill.

250g/8oz shrimps	
1 tsp lemon juice	
1 tbsp finely chopped fresh dill	
8 eggs	
½ tsp salt	
Pinch each of freshly ground black pepper and freshly grated nutmeg	
25g/1 oz butter	
1 dill sprig	

Preparation time: 25 minutes
Nutritional value:
Analysis per serving, approx:
• 1130kJ/270kcal
• 24g protein
• 19g fat
• 0.5g carbohydrate

De-vein the shrimps if necessary, and rinse them under cold water. Pat dry with kitchen paper, sprinkle with lemon juice and mix with the chopped dill. • Beat the eggs with 4 tbsps of water and season with salt, pepper and nutmeg. • Heat 20g/¾oz butter in a pan, then cook a quarter of the egg mixture for 30 seconds to 1 minute over medium heat. The surface should remain shiny and slightly moist. Slip the omelette on to a heated plate and keep hot. Make three more omelettes from the rest of the butter and the remaining egg mixture. Fill the omelettes with the shrimps and garnish with dill. Serve immediately. • A fresh green salad makes a tasty accompaniment.

Our Tip: Omelettes should be served as soon as possible after cooking, so try and use several pans simultaneously.

Extraordinary Fish Hors d'Oeuvres

Spoil your guests with these slimming starters

Fish Soufflé with Millet

Illustrated above left

200g/7oz salmon fillet

1 tbsp lemon juice

Pinch of freshly ground white pepper

$^1/_2$ tsp sea salt

100g/4oz carrots

50g/2oz millet

125ml/4fl oz water

6 tbsps milk

2 eggs

1 tsp finely chopped fresh basil

2 tsps arrowroot

Butter for the dish

Preparation Time: 50 minutes
Baking Time: 30 minutes
Nutritional value:

Analysis per serving, approx:
• 690kJ/165kcal
• 15g protein
• 4g fat
• 16g carbohydrate

If necessary, put the fillet of fish in the freezer compartment of your refrigerator for about 10 minutes to make it easier to cut. • Cut the fish into 5mm/$^1/_4$-inch cubes and toss in the lemon juice, pepper and salt. • Scrape, wash and dice the carrots and cook in a covered pan over a gentle heat in the water with the millet for 10 minutes. Add the milk. Allow the mixture to simmer for a further 10 minutes, then strain off the liquid. • Heat the oven to 200°C/400°F/Gas Mark 6. Grease an ovenproof soufflé dish. • Separate the eggs. Mix the cooked vegetables and millet with the marinated fish, the basil and the egg yolks. Beat the whites until they form stiff peaks, then fold in the arrowroot. Carefully mix the egg white with the fish mixture. • Fill the soufflé dish and bake for 30 minutes. • Serve immediately.

Redfish Fillet with Bean Sprouts

Illustrated above right

300g/10oz redfish or cod fillet

4 tbsps lemon or lime juice

2 tbsps soya sauce

2 pinches freshly ground white pepper

200g/7oz canned bean sprouts

1 tbsp butter

1 tbsp olive oil

2 eggs

100ml/3fl oz cream

1 tsp paprika

3 tbsps chopped chives

Preparation Time: 15 minutes
Nutritional value:

Analysis per serving, approx:
• 1025kJ/245kcal
• 20g protein
• 17g fat
• 2g carbohydrate

Wash the fish, cut into fine strips and mix it with 2 tbsps lemon or lime juice, the soya sauce and the pepper. • Drain the bean sprouts. • Heat the butter and oil in a pan. Fry the bean sprouts for 4 minutes, turning several times. Add the marinated fish and fry it for 3 minutes, stirring regularly. Remove the fish and bean sprouts from the pan and keep them warm. • Beat the eggs with the cream and paprika. Pour this mixture into the pan and stir for 2 minutes while it thickens; stir in 2 tbsps of chopped chives. • Turn the egg out into a heated serving dish. Sprinkle the fish strips and bean sprouts with the remaining lemon juice and spoon them over the egg. Scatter on the remaining chives and serve.

Delicious Hors d'Oeuvres with Shrimp and Scampi

A delight for all lovers of seafood

Scampi au Gratin with Cucumber
Illustrated above left

16 Dublin Bay prawns	
½ cucumber	
2 egg yolks	
2 tbsps white wine	
Salt and freshly ground white pepper	
Pinch of sugar	
125g/5oz well chilled butter	
1 bunch of fresh, or ½tsp dried, tarragon	

Preparation Time: 30 minutes
Nutritional value:
Analysis per serving, approx:
- 1590kJ/380kcal
- 23g protein
- 30g fat
- 3g carbohydrate

Peel, de-vein, rinse and dry the prawns. Peel the cucumber and halve it lengthwise. Scoop out the seeds with a spoon, then cut it into slices. • Butter a flameproof dish and heat the oven to 250°C/450°F/Gas Mark 8. • Fill the dish with the prawns and cucumber. Whisk the egg yolks, wine, salt, pepper and sugar in a bowl standing in warm water, gradually whisking in the flaked butter. Wash the fresh tarragon, chop the leaves finely and stir into the sauce. Pour the sauce over the prawns and cucumber. Bake in the oven for 5 minutes. • A baguette crisped in the oven makes a delicious accompaniment.

Our Tip: Try slices of blanched courgette instead of the cucumber in this gratin.

Vol-au-vents with Shrimp Ragoût
Illustrated above right

125g/5oz mushrooms	
2 tsps lemon juice	
50g/2oz butter	
2 tbsps flour	
125ml/4fl oz hot chicken stock	
125ml/4fl oz dry white wine	
250ml/8fl oz cream	
250g/8oz shrimps	
200g/7oz freshly cooked asparagus tips	
Salt and freshly ground white pepper	
Pinch of sugar	
2 egg yolks	
1 bunch of dill	
4 vol-au-vent cases (frozen)	

Preparation time: 30 minutes
Nutritional value:
Analysis per serving, approx:
- 1670kJ/400kcal • 14g protein
- 31g fat • 10g carbohydrate

Wash and clean the mushrooms, pat them dry and slice thinly; sprinkle with lemon juice and fry in half the butter until the liquid has evaporated. • Prepare a sauce using the remaining butter, the flour, the chicken stock and the wine; allow it to boil for a minute, then add the cream. Add the shrimps, asparagus tips and mushrooms and simmer for a further 5 minutes. • Heat the oven to 200°C/400°F/Gas Mark 6. • Season the ragoût with salt, pepper and sugar. Mix the egg yolks with 2 tbsps of hot sauce. Thicken the ragoût with this mixture but do not allow further boiling. Wash and dry the dill, chop it finely and stir into the ragoût. • Heat the vol-au-vent cases briefly in the oven. Fill with the shrimp ragoût.

Herring Fillets with Spicy Mayonnaise

Every seafood repertoire should include this recipe

4 maatjes herrings
100ml/4fl oz mayonnaise
100ml/4fl oz sour cream
1 bay leaf
6 grains allspice
Pinch each of salt, sugar and freshly ground white pepper
2 onions
2 gherkins
2 sharp apples
1 bunch of dill
Some lettuce leaves

Preparation time: 50 minutes
Nutritional value:
Analysis per serving, approx:
- 2715kJ/650kcal
- 27g protein
- 52g fat
- 18g/3/4oz carbohydrate

Slit the herrings along the belly and clean, taking care to remove the dark membrane. Make a cut in the skin on the back of the fish and pull off the skin, starting at the head. Remove both head and tail, and bone the fish. Soak the fillets in cold water for 30 minutes.
• Meanwhile, mix the sour cream and mayonnaise and add the bay leaf and allspice; season with salt, pepper and sugar. Cut the onion into rings and finely dice the gherkins. Wash, quarter and core the apples, then slice them thinly. Stir the apples, onions and gherkins into the cream and mayonnaise mixture. Wash and dry the dill; reserve a few sprigs for the garnish, then chop the rest finely and stir into the sauce. Remove the bay leaf. • Remove the fillets from the water; dry them and arrange them on a plate. Partially coat the fillets with the sauce and garnish them with the dill, washed lettuce and lemon, apple or onion slices, if desired. Serve the remaining sauce separately.

Sweet and Sour Fish

Piquant, light and with a surprising flavour

500g/1lb 2oz turbot fillets	
Juice of a small lemon	
50g/2oz mushrooms	
100g/4oz canned bamboo shoots	
2 shallots	
4 tbsps sesame oil	
2 tbsps flour	
Salt	
125ml/4fl oz water	
1 tbsp each soya sauce and vinegar	
2 tsps sugar	
1 tbsp cornflour	
1 spring onion	

Preparation time: 45 minutes
Nutritional value:

Analysis per serving, approx:
- 670kJ/160kcal
- 22g protein
- 2g fat
- 12g carbohydrate

Rinse the fish fillets in cold water, dry them and cut them into 3cm/1-inch cubes. Sprinkle with lemon juice. • Wash, clean and dry the mushrooms, then slice them thinly. Drain the bamboo shoots and chop finely. Dice the shallots. • Heat the oil in a large pan. Toss the fish cubes in the flour, sprinkle with salt and fry for 6 minutes, stirring all the time. Place the cooked fish on a dish to keep warm. • Fry the prepared vegetables to a golden brown in the remaining oil. Mix together the water, soya sauce, vinegar, sugar and cornflour; stir into the vegetables and allow to bubble up once. Wash the spring onion and cut into fine strips. Tip the vegetables over the fish cubes and scatter onion strips over them. • Freshly toasted and buttered white bread makes an excellent accompaniment.

Our Tip: Bean sprouts may be used as an alternative to the bamboo shoots.

Bass in Red Sauce

This is best made in a wok or large sauté pan

600g/1lb 6oz bass fillets	
2 shallots	
3 tbsps cornflour	
1 tsp salt	
3 tbsps peanut oil	
125ml/4fl oz water	
$^{1}/_{2}$ tsp vegetable stock granules	
2 tbsps tomato purée	
4 tbsps tomato ketchup	
2 tbsps dry sherry	

Preparation time: 35 minutes
Nutritional value:

Analysis per serving, approx:
- 920kJ/220kcal
- 27g protein
- 8g fat
- 9g carbohydrate

Wash and dry the fish fillets. Cut lengthwise into slices about 5mm/$^{1}/_{4}$ inch thick and crossways into 4cm/2-inch pieces. • Peel and grate the shallots. • Toss the fish slices in a mixture of 2 tbsps cornflour and $^{1}/_{2}$ tsp salt. • Heat the oil in a large pan, stir-fry the fish for 2 or 3 minutes then remove from the pan. • Mix the remaining cornflour with a little water. Bring the water to the boil in a pan. Sprinkle in the stock granules. Stir the grated shallots, the cornflour paste, tomato purée and ketchup into the stock and bring to the boil. • Season this sauce with salt and add the sherry. • Add the fish in the sauce, but do not allow it to cook further. • Serve with firm boiled rice.

New Hors d'Oeuvre Ideas

Fresh, vitamin-rich dishes – piquant and fascinating

Stuffed Avocados
Illustrated left

50g/2oz millet
$^{1}/_{2}$ tsp sea salt
4 tbsps milk
100g/4oz shelled peas
2 hard-boiled eggs
50g/2oz smoked salmon
2 fully ripe avocados
1 tbsp sunflower oil
1 tbsp each lemon juice and cream
2 pinches five-spice powder
Pinch of white pepper
1 tbsp each chopped chives and chopped parsley

Preparation time: 30 minutes
Nutritional value:
Analysis per serving, approx:
- 1695kJ/405kcal • 11g protein
- 32g fat • 17g carbohydrate

Boil the millet with the salt and 125ml/4fl oz water for 10 minutes in a covered pan. Add the milk and the peas and cook for 10 minutes until tender; strain through a sieve. • Slice the eggs and cut the salmon into fine strips. Halve the avocados, remove the stone and hollow the fruit out a little more with a teaspoon. Mix the egg slices, salmon strips and avocado flesh with the remaining ingredients. Fill the avocado halves with the mixture.

Spring Cocktail
Illustrated above centre

100g/4oz young spinach
1 shallot
200ml/4fl oz low-fat quark
200ml/4fl oz crème fraîche
150g/5$^{1}/_{2}$oz shrimps
2 tsps soya sauce
$^{1}/_{2}$tsp paprika • 2 tbsps chopped chives
1 bunch of radishes

Preparation time: 15 minutes

Nutritional value:
Analysis per serving, approx:
- 1085kJ/260kcal • 17g protein
- 18g fat • 6g carbohydrate

Wash the spinach and separate the leaves and stalks; divide between four cocktail glasses. • Peel and finely chop the shallots, and mix with the quark, crème fraîche, shrimps, soy sauce, paprika and 1tbsp chives. Spoon the mixture onto the spinach; garnish with the radishes and the remaining chives.

Coley with Spinach
Illustrated above right

250g/8oz spinach
250g/8oz coley fillet
2 tbsps lemon juice
Pinch of pepper
2 tbsps olive oil
3 hard-boiled eggs
1 tbsp soya sauce
1 tomato
1 slice bread
1 tbsp chopped chives

Preparation time: 30 minutes
Nutritional value:
Analysis per serving, approx:
- 835kJ/200kcal • 19g protein
- 10gfat
- 7g carbohydrate

Wash the spinach and chop coarsely. • Rinse the fish and season with 1 tbsp lemon juice and the pepper; cover and steam in the oil and 1 tablespoon of water for 5 minutes. Turn the fish, scatter with a sprinkling of spinach leaves and cook for a further 5 minutes. • Break up the fish. Slice the egg and reserve four slices. Stir the fish pieces, egg slices, soya sauce and remaining lemon juice into the spinach. • Garnish with the remaining egg, some small tomato wedges, toast and chives. Serve hot.

Classic Seafood Cocktails for Festive Occasions

A deliciously traditional way to start a special meal

Prawn Cocktail
Illustrated above left

16 king prawns
4 lettuce leaves
125ml/4fl oz mayonnaise
3-4 tbsps tomato ketchup
1-2 tbsps dry sherry
Juice of half a lemon
Pinch each of salt and sugar
1/2 tsp white pepper

Preparation time: 15 minutes
Nutritional value:
Analysis per slice, approx:
• 940kJ/225kcal
• 9g protein
• 17g fat
• 9g carbohydrate

Peel and de-vein the prawns. Rinse under cold running water and dry. • Wash the lettuce leaves; line four cocktail glasses with the dried leaves. • Make the sauce using the mayonnaise and the remaining ingredients. Pour into the lined glasses. Hang four prawns from the rim of each glass, to be dipped in the sauce.

Shrimp Cocktail
Illustrated above centre

24 shrimps in their shells
100g/4oz mushrooms
Juice of 1 lemon
Pinch each of salt, white pepper and sugar
3 tbsps mayonnaise
1 lettuce heart
100g/4oz freshly cooked asparagus tips

Preparation time: 20 minutes
Nutritional value:
Analysis per serving, approx:
• 670kJ/170kcal
• 18g protein
• 8g fat
• 4g carbohydrate

Peel and de-vein the shrimps; rinse under cold running water and drain. • Clean the mushrooms and slice finely. Mix together the lemon juice, salt, pepper, sugar and mayonnaise. Break the lettuce into leaves, wash, dry and cut into strips. Mix the shrimps, asparagus tips, lettuce strips and mushrooms together with the sauce. • Serve in four cocktail glasses.

Lobster Cocktail
Illustrated above right

1 small frozen lobster
1/2 bunch dill
Juice of 1/2 lemon
3 tbsps mayonnaise
Salt and freshly ground white pepper
Pinch of sugar
Few lettuce leaves of your choice
4 dill sprigs
1/2 lemon

Thawing time: 12 hours
Preparation time: 20 minutes
Nutritional value:
Analysis per serving, approx:
• 630kJ/150kcal
• 4g protein
• 13g fat
• 3g carbohydrate

Remove the lobster from its packaging and thaw in a refrigerator. • Scoop out the flesh and cut it into thin slices. Wash, dry and chop the dill. • Mix together the lemon juice and mayonnaise; season with salt, pepper and sugar. • Stir the lobster meat into the sauce, then mix in the dill. • Wash and dry the lettuce; line a salad bowl with the leaves. Arrange the cocktail in the bowl. Decorate with washed dill sprigs, half slices of lemon and the lobster claws.

Hors d' Oeuvres for Special Occasions

Fine ingredients, carefully prepared and beutifully presented

Gravad Lax
Illustrated above left

To serve 8:

1kg/2¼lbs fresh salmon (centre cut if possible)
1½ tbsps caster sugar
2 tbsps coarse salt
1 tsp freshly ground white pepper
3 bunches dill • 1 lemon

Preparation time: 20 minutes
Marinating time: at least 2 days
Nutritional value:
Analysis per serving, approx:
• 1130kJ/270kcal • 25g protein
• 17g fat • 4g carbohydrate

Cut the salmon in half lengthways; remove the backbone and, using tweezers, also remove all the smaller bones. Dry the salmon fillets with kitchen paper. • Combine the salt and sugar. Sprinkle a little of the mixture into a deep square glass or porcelain dish and place one fillet, skin side down, in the dish. Cover the salmon with a good sprinkling of the sugar and salt mixture, then grind some white pepper over the top. Wash and dry the dill, chop finely and scatter over the fillet. Lay the other half of the salmon over the first and sprinkle with more sugar-salt mixture. Cover the salmon with aluminium foil, then place a board on top. Place a weight, a can or similar heavy object, on top. • Leave the salmon in a cool place for at least two days, turning several times during this period. • To serve, place the salmon, skin downwards, on a board, scrape off the dill and seasonings then slice the salmon thinly towards the tail end. Garnish with lemon. • The salmon should be served with a sweet mustard-and-dill mayonnaise made with 4 tbsps hot mustard, 3 tbsps caster sugar, 2 tbsps wine vinegar, 5 tbsps oil and 4 tbsps chopped dill.

Smoked Trout with Horseradish Sauce
Illustrated above right

350g/11oz celery
1 tbsp lemon juice
2 smoked trout
125ml/4fl oz cream
40g/11½oz freshly grated horseradish
Pinch each of salt and sugar
1 untreated lemon

Preparation time: 40 minutes
Nutritional value:
Analysis per serving, approx:
• 940kJ/220kcal
• 22g protein
• 13g fat
• 6g carbohydrate

Break the celery into sticks. Trim the root end and the leaves and discard them. Slice the rest into matchstick-sized strips.

Arrange the shredded celery on a plate and sprinkle with the lemon juice. • Skin and fillet the trout, removing the smaller bones as you do so. Halve the fillets and arrange into a star shape on the celery bed. • Whip the cream until stiff, add the horseradish and season with the salt and sugar. Take a piping bag with a large star-shaped nozzle and fill it with the cream. Decorate each trout fillet with a small amount of the mixture. • Wash and dry the lemon. Cut thin slices from the centre of the fruit and use as a garnish.

Spiny Lobster Tails with Melon

Unusual pleasures for festive occasions

4 frozen spiny lobster tails, 200g/7oz each	
4 tomatoes	
2 shallots	
1 onion	
1 stick celery	
1 fresh tarragon sprig	
1 small honeydew melon	
1 bay leaf	
1 tbsp caraway seed	
Salt	
4 drops Tabasco sauce	
2 egg yolks	
2 tbsps prepared hot mustard	
4 tbsps oil	
4 tbsps cognac	
125ml/4fl oz cream	
1 small piece of tinned truffle (optional)	

Thawing time: 8 hours
Preparation time: 1 hour
Nutritional value:
Analysis per serving, approx:
- 1880kJ/450kcal • 16g protein
- 24g fat • 35g carbohydrate

Thaw the lobster tails in the refrigerator for about 8 hours.
• Skin the tomatoes and slice them into eighths. Dice the onions and shallots. Wash the celery and tarragon; slice the celery and chop the tarragon finely. Cut the melon in half and remove the pips. Hollow out the flesh with a melon-baller and mix the flesh with the tomatoes, tarragon and shallots. Chill the mixture. • Boil the onion, celery, bay leaf, caraway, 1 tbsp salt and Tabasco sauce for 5 minutes in 1l/1³/₄ pints of water. Place the lobster tails in the pan and cook for 5 minutes over a low heat until tender; leave them in the liquid to cool. • Beat the egg yolks with the mustard and some salt. Mix in the oil drop by drop with half the cognac and a little truffle juice, if using. Whip the cream until stiff and combine with the cognac liquid. • Arrange the salad in the melon halves. Cut the lobster tails in half lengthways. Scrape out the flesh and arrange it in the shells, decorate with small slices of truffle and sprinkle with the remaining cognac. Serve with the mustard mayonnaise.

Special Salmon Mousse

This mousse should be prepared as soon as possible before serving

To serve 6:

500g/1lb 2oz fresh salmon fillets
25g/1oz butter
Salt
Freshly ground white pepper
6 tbsps olive oil
Juice of 1 lemon
4 tbsps dry sherry
Pinch cayenne pepper
200ml/6fl oz whipping cream
2 dill sprigs

Preparation time: 40 minutes
Chilling time: 1 hour
Nutritional value:
Analysis per serving, approx:
• 1595kJ/380kcal
• 18g protein
• 35g fat
• 3g carbohydrate

Wash the salmon fillets in cold water and pat dry. • Heat the butter in a large pan. Chill a suitable mould in the refrigerator. Rub the fillets with salt and pepper, fry on each side for about half a minute. Remove from the pan and wrap in aluminium foil while still hot.Allow the fillets to cool in the foil. • All other ingredients should be at room temperature before use. • Remove any remaining bones from the cooled fillets and cut the fish into bite-sized pieces. • Mix the olive oil with the lemon juice, sherry, salt and cayenne pepper, then purée with the fish pieces in a food processor. Switch the food processor off every few seconds, and let the mixture rest before switching on again; during a continuous operation the machine may become too warm and cause the mixture to become runny. • Whip the cream until stiff and combine it with the mousse. Fill a chilled mould with the mousse and leave to solidify in the refrigerator. • When it is time to serve the mousse, turn it out onto a dish, slice and serve garnished with dill.

Fish and Asparagus in Aspic

Refreshing when made with delicate spring vegetables

250g/8oz asparagus
100g/4oz shelled peas
250ml/9fl oz water
4 tsps vegetable stock granules
Freshly ground white pepper
200g/7oz redfish or other white fish fillet
3 tsps lemon juice
1 hard-boiled egg
2 pinches five-spice powder
2 tsps finely chopped dill
1 tsp agar agar

Preparation time: 1 hour
Nutritional value:
Analysis per serving, approx:
• 480kJ/115kcal
• 13g protein
• 4g fat
• 6g carbohydrate

Wash the asparagus and peel it starting at the head and cut it into 2cm/³/₄ -inch pieces. Bring the water to the boil and add the asparagus, the peas, 2 tsps of stock granules and the pepper. Wash the fillet of fish and sprinkle with 1 tbsp lemon juice. Place the fish on the vegetables in the pan, cover and cook for 10 minutes or until tender. • Remove the fish and vegetables from the pan with a slotted spoon. Break the fish into pieces and mix it carefully with the vegetables. Arrange it in four glass dishes. Slice the egg into 8 wedges and top each portion with them. • Season the fish and vegetable liquid with the lemon juice, the remaining stock granules and the five-spice powder. Add the dill. Slowly sprinkle in the agar agar and stir with a whisk. Cover the pan and heat for 10 minutes but do not allow to boil. Pour the liquid evenly over the fish and vegetables and leave to cool.

Scallops au Gratin

Keep the shells as a container for other hors d'oeuvres!

4 fresh scallops
1 shallot
50g/2oz spinach
100g/4oz mushrooms
75g/3oz butter
125ml/4fl oz white wine
4 tbsps double cream
Salt
4 tbsps breadcrumbs
2 tbsps freshly grated cheese

Preparation time: 1 hour
Nutritional value:
Analysis per serving, approx:
• 2070kJ/495kcal
• 35g protein
• 29g fat
• 17g carbohydrate

Break open the scallop shells, remove the white flesh and the orange coral and rinse. Clean the shells and boil them for a few minutes. • Chop the shallots finely. Wash the spinach thoroughly, drain well and chop finely. Clean and dry the mushrooms and slice thinly. • Heat 50g/2oz of the butter. Fry the mussel flesh and the coral briefly, remove from the pan and keep hot. Fry the chopped shallot in the butter until it becomes transparent. Add the spinach and mushrooms and heat for 5 minutes. • Add the wine and double cream and bring to the boil; season with salt. Return the mussel flesh and the coral to the pan and reheat for a short time. • Heat the oven to 220°C/ 450°F/Gas Mark 8. • Spoon the mixture into the scallop shells, mix the breadcrumbs with the cheese, and scatter this mixture over the scallop sauce. Cut the rest of the butter into small pieces and dot the mixture with it. • Bake the scallops on the top shelf of the oven for about 10 minutes or until a crisp golden crust has formed.

King Prawns in Garlic Butter

This dish is quick to prepare

2 cloves garlic
Salt
1 bunch of parsley
125g/5oz softened butter
Freshly ground black pepper
1/2 tsp lemon juice
12 king prawns
1 small untreated lemon

Preparation time: 15 minutes
Cooking time: 15 minutes
Nutritional value:
Analysis per serving, approx:
• 1695kJ/405kcal
• 32g protein
• 30g fat
• 2g carbohydrate

Chop the garlic cloves coarsely, sprinkle with salt, then crush. Wash, dry and finely chop the parsley; reserve 1 tbsp of it. Mix the butter with the garlic, parsley, pepper and lemon juice. • Coat a flameproof dish with half the butter mixture. Heat the oven to 240°C/450°F/Gas Mark 8. •

Wash the prawns thoroughly and remove the heads. Using a sharp knife, de-vein the prawns. Pat them dry them, arrange them in the dish and scatter the remaining parsley over them. • Bake the prawns on the middle shelf of the oven for 10-15 minutes or until they are crisp and red on the outside. • Wash, dry and slice the lemon. Serve the prawns garnished with the rest of the parsley and half slices of lemon. • Fresh, crisp French bread and a well-chilled white wine make a delicious accompaniment.

Variations on Oysters for the Connoisseur

Anyone who enjoys oysters will love them cooked as well as raw

Deep-fried Oysters
Illustrated above left

48 fresh oysters
1/2 bunch of parsley
4 tbsps breadcrumbs
White pepper
1 egg yolk
4 tbsps flour
Some lettuce leaves
1 untreated lemon
1l/1³/4 pints oil for frying

Preparation time: 50 minutes
Nutritional value:
Analysis per serving, approx:
• 3260kJ/780kcal • 59g protein
• 33g fat • 58g carbohydrate

Open the oysters and remove the flesh from the shell with the point of a knife. Pat the oysters dry. • Wash and dry the parsley, chop finely and mix with the breadcrumbs and pepper.

Beat the egg yolk. • Toss the oysters first in flour, then in the egg yolk and finally in the breadcrumbs. • Heat the oil in a deep fryer. Deep-fry the oysters in batches for about 2 minutes until golden brown; keep them warm. Serve on lettuce leaves, garnished with slices of lemon.

Our Tip: Instead of oysters you could use fresh or canned mussels.

Oysters Kilpatrick
Illustrated above centre

75g/3oz back bacon rashers, rinds discarded
24 fresh oysters
Few drops of Worcestershire sauce
1 untreated lemon

Preparation time: 20 minutes
Nutritional value:
Analysis per serving, approx:
• 870kJ/205kcal • 27g protein

• 4g fat • 16g carbohydrate

Slice the bacon into thin strips. Shuck the oysters open with an oyster knife or strong kitchen knife. • Heat the grill to 250°C/450°F/Gas Mark 8. • Place the oysters on a baking sheet. Top with the bacon strips and Worcestershire sauce. Grill the oysters until the bacon is crisp. • Serve with lemon wedges.

Oysters Rockefeller
Illustrated above right

500g/1lb 2oz young spinach
1 each onion and garlic clove
30g/1oz butter
Pinch each of salt, white pepper and freshly grated nutmeg
16 fresh oysters
4 tbsps crème fraîche
Cayenne pepper
1 tbsp grated Pecorino cheese

Preparation time: 40 minutes
Nutritional value:
Analysis per serving, approx:
• 1235kJ/295kcal
• 26g protein
• 14g fat
• 16g carbohydrate

Wash the spinach. Chop the onion and garlic finely and fry it briefly in the butter. Cook the spinach until it wilts and add the seasonings. Cook for 2 minutes then remove from the heat and drain. • Heat the grill or oven to 250°C/450°F/Gas Mark 8. • Butter four small flameproof dishes and fill them with the drained spinach. Shuck the oysters and empty them, with their liquid, into the dishes. • Mix the crème fraîche with salt and cayenne pepper and the Pecorino. Top the oysters with the mixture and bake or grill until lightly browned.

Magnificently Presented Lobsters

The availability of frozen lobster should encourage you to try these at home

Lobster au Gratin
Illustrated above left

2 frozen lobsters, each weighing 500g/1lb 2oz
4 shallots
200g/7oz mushrooms
375ml/15fl oz cream
100g/4oz butter
2 tsps flour
2 tbsps olive oil
1 tsp salt
White pepper
1 bunch dill
50g/2oz freshly grated Cheddar cheese
3 tbsps dry breadcrumbs

Thawing time: 10 hours
Preparation time: 1 hour
Nutritional value:
Analysis per serving, approx:
• 1610kJ/310kcal
• 23g protein
• 26g fat
• 13g carbohydrate

Thaw the lobster for 10 hours in the refrigerator. • Halve the lobster, scoop out the flesh and cut it into 3cm/1-inch cubes. • Chop the shallots finely. Wash the mushrooms and slice thinly, place in a pan with the shallots and cream and reduce to one third of the original volume. Mix the flour with 30g/1oz butter to make the flour and butter paste called beurre manié. • Heat the oil, add 50g/2oz butter and the lobster meat, season with salt and pepper and fry for 2 minutes. • Heat the oven to 220°C/450°F/Gas Mark 8. • Wash, dry and finely chop the dill, and stir it into the sauce with the beurre manié. Cook for 2 minutes, season and mix with the lobster meat. Fill the lobster shells with the sauce, sprinkle with cheese and breadcrumbs and top with the remaining butter in flakes. • Bake for 10-15 minutes until golden brown.

Lobster Dijonnaise
Illustrated above right

2 frozen lobsters, each weighing 500g/1lb 2oz
1 tsp salt
2 tsps paprika
4 shallots
2 tbsps olive oil
100g/4oz butter
4 tbsps cognac
4 tbsps fino sherry
375ml/15fl oz cream
Juice of half a lemon
2 tsps Dijon mustard
Pinch of cayenne pepper
2 egg yolks
Some basil leaves

Thawing time: 10 hours
Preparation time: 1½ hours
Nutritional value:
Analysis per serving, approx:
• 2760kJ/660kcal • 43g protein
• 45g fat • 7g carbohydrate

Allow the lobster to thaw for about 10 hours in the refrigerator. • Break off the claws and break them open with the back of a kitchen chopper. Halve the lobsters lengthways. Remove the cartilage and the vein from the tail. Scoop the meat out of the tail, body and claws, and sprinkle with salt and paprika. Finely chop the shallots. • Heat the butter with the oil and fry the lobster meat for 5 minutes, fry the shallots for 1 minute with the meat, then add the sherry and cognac and cook gently for another minute. Remove the lobster meat and keep hot. • Pour the cream into the pan and reduce the liquid by about a half. • Blend the lemon juice, mustard, cayenne pepper and egg yolks in a liquidiser and stir it into the cream sauce; season as necessary. • Coat the lobster meat with the sauce and garnish with basil.

Exquisite Main Courses

Light meals, hearty hotpots and baked or steamed fish make for a varied range of meals

Devilled Cod Fillets with Broccoli and Tomatoes

Simple, quick and delicious

Fillet of Fish Florentine

Poached fish fillet on spinach is a dish from nothern Italy

4 cod fillets (800g/1lb 12oz)	
2 lemons	
2 tsps hot mustard	
Salt and freshly ground black pepper	
3 tbsps flour • 1 egg	
4 tbsps breadcrumbs	
65g/2½oz butter	
400g/14oz tomatoes	
½ tsp each salt and freshly ground black pepper	
500g/1lb 2oz broccoli	
1 onion	

Preparation time: 30 minutes
Nutritional value:

Analysis per serving, approx:
• 1775kJ/425kcal • 43g protein
• 18g fat • 22g carbohydrate

Rinse the fillets in cold water, then dry them and sprinkle them with juice from 1 lemon. Leave to marinate for a few minutes. Dab them dry, spread with mustard and sprinkle with salt. Toss the fillets one by one in flour, beaten egg and finally in the breadcrumbs. Fry the breaded fillets in 25g/1oz of the butter for about 5 minutes on either side, then arrange on a heated plate and keep warm. • Cut a cross in the tomatoes top and bottom and, holding them on a fork, immerse in boiling water, then skin and remove the hard knot where the stalk joins the fruit. • Heat 15g/1½oz of the butter, place the tomatoes in the pan and sprinkle them with salt and pepper. Cut 15g/½oz of the butter into tiny pieces and scatter them over the top. Cook for 10 minutes. • Wash and clean the broccoli and cut a cross in the ends of the stalks. Finely chop the onion and fry in the remaining butter until transparent. Add the broccoli and a sprinkling of salt and cook for 10 minutes over a gentle heat together with 125ml/4fl oz of water and 2 tbsps lemon juice. •Arrange the vegetables around the fish. Garnish with lemon.

750g/1lb 10oz young spinach	
2 onions	
1 untreated lemon	
100g/4oz Bel Paese or similar full-fat cheese	
125ml/4fl oz white wine	
1 bay leaf	
½ bunch parsley	
800g/1lb 12oz redfish fillet	
2 tbsps oil	
½ tsp salt	
Pinch each of freshly ground white pepper and freshly grated nutmeg	

Preparation time: 1¼ hours
Nutritional value:

Analysis per serving, approx:
• 1965kJ/470kcal
• 50g protein
• 22g fat
• 11g carbohydrate

Pick over the spinach and discard any yellow leaves and coarse stalks. Wash the spinach thoroughly several times. Chop the onion finely. Wash the lemon and slice thinly. Grate the cheese, or if it is too soft, chop it into small pieces. • Heat the wine, bay leaf and parsley in a large pan. Wash the fillets and add them to the liquid. Cover and cook over a low heat for 15 minutes. • Heat the oven to 220°C/450°F/Gas Mark 8. Butter a shallow flameproof dish. • Fry the onions in oil until they turn yellow, add the moist spinach and season with salt, pepper and nutmeg; cover and cook for 10 minutes. • Drain the spinach through a sieve and reserve the liquid. Arrange overlapping bands of fish and spinach across the dish. • Add the spinach juice to the fish liquid. Reduce this stock by half over a high flame, then pour over the fish. Top with lemon slices and scatter cheese over the top. • Bake for 7-10 minutes.

Fish Rolls in Herb Sauce

A fine fish fillet and aromatic herbs complement one another perfectly

500g/1lb 2oz small plaice or sole fillets
3 tbsps lemon juice
2 tsps garlic salt
3 tbsps each finely chopped lemon balm, dill and parsley or chervil
40g/1½oz butter
1 fennel bulb (about 250g/8oz)
125ml/4fl oz each water and white wine
1 tsp vegetable stock granules
4 tbsps ground rice
100ml/3fl oz single cream

Preparation time: 30 minutes
Nutritional value:
Analysis per serving, approx:
• 1570kJ/375kcal
• 24g protein
• 21g fat
• 15g carbohydrate

Wash and dry the fillets and sprinkle 2 tbsps lemon juice and a little garlic salt on each side. Scatter three quarters of the chopped mixed herbs over the fish fillets and place a flake of butter in the centre of each. Roll the fillets up and secure with a wooden cocktail stick. • Clean the fennel bulb and cut it in four; fry the fennel in the remaining butter over a low heat for 2 or 3 minutes, stirring constantly. Add the water, wine and stock granules, cover and cook for 10 minutes. • Add the rice and stir it into the liquid. Place the fish rolls in the pan and poach over a low heat for 7 minutes. • Combine the cream with the lemon juice and the remaining herbs. Remove the pan from the heat. • Arrange the fish rolls on a heated dish. Thicken the sauce with the cream, season with garlic salt and pour over the fish. • Coarse brown rice or mashed potatoes and a green salad make a good · accompaniment.

Cuttlefish and Squid

Available both ready-cooked and frozen

Squid with Tomatoes
Illustrated above foreground

750g/1lb 10oz frozen squid
3 onions
2 cloves garlic
1 small fennel bulb
1 small carrot
4 tbsps olive oil
100g/4oz butter
1 tsp salt
Freshly ground white pepper
4 tbsps brandy
4 large beefsteak tomatoes
1 tsp freshly chopped thyme

Thawing time: about 1¹/₂ hours
Preparation time: 1 hour
Nutritional value:
Analysis per serving, approx:
• 2110kJ/505kcal
• 32g protein
• 33g fat
• 15g carbohydrate

Remove the squid from its packaging and thaw in the refrigerator for about 1¹/₂ hours; wash and dry it. • Clean the fennel, scrape the carrot and finely chop the fennel, carrot, onion and garlic. • Heat the oil and add the squid and half the butter; season with salt and pepper and fry for about 5 minutes until golden brown. Pour the brandy over the squid and remove the pan from the heat. • Warm the rest of the butter, add the vegetables, cover and heat for 10 minutes over a gentle heat. Skin the tomatoes and cut them into eighths; remove the tough part where the stalk joins the fruit. Add the tomatoes, the thyme and the cooked vegetables to the squid. • Cover and, depending on the size of the squid, braise them for 20 to 25 minutes. • Delicious with boiled rice or French bread.

Deep-fried Cuttlefish
Illustrated above in background

500g/1lb 2oz frozen cuttlefish
Black pepper
2 lemons
1 tsp freshly chopped thyme
1 tbsp olive oil
150g flour
¹/₂ tsp dried yeast
2 eggs
125ml/4fl oz white wine
¹/₂ tsp salt
Oil for frying

Thawing time: 1¹/₂ hours
Preparation time: 1 hour
Nutritional value:
Analysis per serving, approx:
• 2195kJ/525kcal
• 26g protein
• 31g fat
• 29g carbohydrate

Thaw the cuttlefish for about 1¹/₂ hours. • Wash under cold water, pat dry and slice into rings. Squeeze the juice from one of the lemons. Toss the cuttlefish rings in a mixture of pepper, lemon juice, thyme and olive oil. Cover, and marinate at room temperature for about 30 minutes. • Sift the flour into a bowl and mix with the dried yeast. Separate the egg yolks from the whites. Mix the egg yolks, wine and salt into the flour. Beat the egg whites until they form stiff peaks, stir them into the batter, cover, and leave to stand for 15 minutes. • Heat the oil to 175°C/350°F in a deep-fryer. Use a fork to dip the cuttlefish rings in the batter and fry in batches until they are golden brown all over. • Drain the fried rings on absorbent paper and keep them warm. • Arrange the rings on a serving dish and garnish with lemon wedges. • French bread and a green salad round the meal off nicely.

Curried Prawns

An Indian dish with an interesting, orginal flavour

1 onion	
1 clove garlic	
3 tbsps butter	
1-2 tbsps flour	
2 tsps Madras curry powder	
250ml/8fl oz hot chicken stock	
250ml/8fl oz water	
1 small banana	
4 tbsps single cream	
Pinch each of salt, freshly ground white pepper and powdered ginger	
$^1/_2$-1tsp lemon juice	
400g/14oz prawns	
2 tbsps almond flakes	

Preparation time: 30 minutes
Nutritional value:

Analysis per serving, approx:
- 1150kJ/275kcal
- 19g protein
- 16g fat
- 14g carbohydrate

Chop the onion and garlic very finely and fry in the butter until transparent. Stir in the flour and curry powder, and dilute with the chicken stock and water. Simmer the sauce for 5 minutes. • Peel and mash the banana and stir into the sauce. Thicken the sauce with the cream and season with salt, pepper, ginger and lemon juice. • De-vein the prawns if necessary; wash them in cold water, dry on kitchen paper and heat them in the sauce. • Toast the almond flakes in a dry pan until golden brown, scatter them over the curry and serve immediately. • Delicious with buttered long-grain rice or French bread and fresh green salad.

Fish Fricassée

Cucumber, onions and fish - a perfect combination

3 onions	
50g butter	
600g/1lb 6oz cucumber	
2 tsps garlic salt	
2 pinches freshly ground white pepper	
500g/1lb 2oz cod fillet	
3 tbsps lemon juice	
100ml/3fl oz cream	
2 tbsps wholemeal flour	
1 tsp five-spice or $^1/_2$ tsp curry powder	
1 tbsp finely chopped fresh dill	
1 tsp fresh basil leaves cut into strips	

Preparation time: 30 minutes
Nutritional value:

Analysis per serving, approx:
- 1400kJ/335kcal
- 25g protein
- 19g fat
- 15g carbohydrate

Chop the onion coarsely. Heat the butter in a large pan. Fry the onions over a gentle heat until transparent. • Peel and dice the cucumber, add to the onions and sprinkle with 1 tsp garlic salt and a pinch of pepper. Cook the vegetables for 10 minutes. • Wash and dry the fillet of fish, sprinkle with 1 tbsp of lemon juice and the remaining pepper. Cut the fish into large chunks, scatter it over the vegetables and simmer over a gentle heat for 5-7 minutes. • Combine the cream with the flour and five-spice or curry powder. Thicken the fricassée and allow to cook for a further minute. Carefully stir the herbs into the fricassée; season with garlic salt, the remaining lemon juice and more five-spice if necessary. • Excellent with mashed potatoes or brown rice.

47

Maatjes Fillets with Green Beans

A simple but filling meal

Halibut Steaks in Caper Sauce

Fish with caper sauce - a combination that has stood the test of time

8 maatjes herring fillets
750g/1lb 10 oz green beans
750ml/1¼ pints water
1 tsp salt
1 bunch savory
100g/4oz streaky bacon
1 bunch parsley
6 onions

Preparation time: 50 minutes
Nutritional value:

Analysis per serving, approx:
- 2425kJ/580kcal
- 22g protein
- 45g fat
- 21g carbohydrate

Depending on their salt content, soak the maatjes herrings for 20-30 minutes. • Wash and clean the beans, removing any strings as you do so. Bring the salted water to the boil and boil the beans with the savory for 15 minutes. • Finely dice the bacon. Strain the beans (reserve the liquid for other dishes if desired) and keep warm. Wash, dry and finely chop the parsley and stir into the beans. Fry the bacon in a pan until crispy. Chop 3 onions into cubes and fry until golden brown in the bacon fat, stirring constantly. Cut the remaining onions into paper-thin rings. • Dry the maatjes herrings. Spread some ice cubes on a dish, arrange the maatjes fillets and garnish with onion rings. Serve with the hot beans and bacon-onion mixture. • New potatoes taste best of all with this dish.

4 halibut steaks, 200g/7oz each
Juice of 1 lemon
250ml/8fl oz each water and white wine
1 tbsp vinegar
½ tbsp salt
1 onion
4 each peppercorns and allspice grains
1 bay leaf
2 tbsps butter
1 tbsp flour
1 tbsp capers
Pinch each of salt and sugar
1 egg yolk
2 tbsps cream
½ lemon

Preparation time: 15 minutes
Cooking time: 30 minutes
Nutritional value:

Analysis per serving, approx:
- 1485kJ/355kcal
- 22g protein
- 41g fat
- 14g carbohydrate

Rinse the halibut steaks, pat them dry, sprinkle with lemon juice and leave to stand for 10 minutes. • In a large pan boil up the water, wine vinegar, salt, onion, pepper, allspice and bay leaf for 5 minutes. Place the steaks in the stock and leave over a gentle heat for 15 minutes. • Place the steaks on a heated serving dish and set aside; strain the stock. • Melt the butter in a pan, fry the flour until it starts to colour, stirring constantly, then add the fish stock. Bring the sauce to the boil. • Mix the capers into the sauce and season with salt and sugar. Beat the egg yolk into the cream and then stir in 2 tbsps of the sauce. Remove the pan from the heat and thicken the sauce with the cream and egg mixture. • Wash and slice the lemon. Pour the sauce over the steaks and garnish with lemon slices.

Rolled Fillets in Piquant Sauces

The delicate flavour of fish permits any number of variations

Rolled Fish with Sliced Apple
Illustrated above left

750g/1lb10oz filleted fish (cod or redfish) sliced as thinly as possible into 8 strips

Juice of 1 lemon

Salt and pepper

2 tbsps sour cream

4 tbsps freshly chopped parsley

1 onion

40g/1¹/₂oz butter

2 tbsps flour

¹/₂-1 tbsp curry powder

500ml/16fl oz hot vegetable stock

2 large apples

1 tbsp breadcrumbs

Preparation time: 40 minutes
Nutritional value:
Analysis per serving, approx:
• 1420kJ/340kcal
• 34g protein
• 12g fat
• 23g carbohydrate

Wash and dry the fillets, sprinkle them with the lemon juice and allow to stand for a few minutes. Season with salt and pepper, spread with sour cream and sprinkle with parsley. Roll up the fillets and secure with wooden cocktail sticks. • Chop the onions very finely and fry in the butter until transparent. Stir in the flour and curry and add the vegetable stock. Bring the sauce to the boil and season with salt and sugar. Place the fish rolls in the sauce over a low heat for 15 minutes. • Peel the apples, cut four thick slices from the centre of each and remove the core. Toss the slices in the breadcrumbs, fry until nearly soft in the butter, and place on a dish to keep warm. • Arrange the apple slices on a dish and pour the sauce over them. • Delicious with boiled long-grain rice.

Fish Rolls in Tomato Sauce
Illustrated above right

750g/1lb10oz filleted fish (cod, coley or redfish), sliced as thinly as possible

Juice of 1 lemon

40g/1¹/₄oz thinly sliced streaky bacon

2 onions

1 small bunch parsley

1 tbsp mustard

2 tbsps butter

2 tbsps tomato purée

250ml/8fl oz hot vegetable stock

Pinch each of salt, freshly ground white pepper and sugar

100ml/3fl oz crème fraîche

Some basil leaves

Preparation time: 1 hour
Nutritional value:
Analysis per serving, approx:
• 1525kJ/365kcal
• 36g protein
• 21g fat
• 8g carbohydrate

Wash and dry the fish fillets and sprinkle them with lemon juice. • Cut the bacon rashers in half along their length and fry to a light brown. Finely chop the onion. Wash, dry and finely chop the parsley. • Spread the fish fillets with mustard, scatter with the chopped onion and parsley and top each with a strip of bacon. Roll up the fillets and secure with a wooden cocktail stick. • Heat the butter. Stir in the tomato purée and top up with vegetable stock. Bring the sauce to the boil, season with salt, pepper and sugar and thicken with crème fraîche. • Place the fish rolls in the sauce for 15 minutes. Garnish with basil leaves.

Plaice Fillets on Brown Rice

Brown rice requires longer cooking than white rice, but has a lovely, nutty flavour

200g/7oz long-grain brown rice
500ml/16fl oz water
1 tbsp vegetable stock granules
1 tsp five-spice powder
500g/1lb 2oz cucumber
Freshly ground white pepper
200ml/6fl oz whipping cream
3 tbsps lemon juice
1 egg
2 tbsps finely chopped fresh dill
500g/1lb 2oz plaice fillets
1 untreated lemon
1 tomato

Preparation time: 45 minutes
Nutritional value:
Analysis per serving, approx:
- 2050kJ/490kcal
- 30g protein
- 19g fat
- 43g carbohydrate

Boil the rice for 15 minutes over a gentle heat in a large pan containing the water, stock granules and five-spice powder. • Peel and dice the cucumber, mix with the rice and season with a pinch of pepper. Cover and cook for a further 15 minutes. • Whip the cream with 2 tbsps of the lemon juice, the egg and 1 tbsp of dill. •Wash the fish, sprinkle with the remaining pepper and lay the fish on the rice. Pour the cream over the top and cook for a further 10 minutes over a very gentle heat. • Remove the pan from the heat. Sprinkle the rest of the dill and lemon juice over the fish. • Wash and dry the lemon and tomato, cut them into wedges or slices, and use to garnish the dish.

Our Tip: Diced courgette may be used as a substitute for the cucumber.

Classic Trout Dishes

Classic recipes for this delicious freshwater fish

Trout au Bleu
Illustrated above left

4 fresh trout	
1 tsp salt	
125ml/4fl oz wine vinegar	
3l/4 pints water	
2 tsps salt	
125ml/4fl oz dry white wine	
125g/5oz butter	
1 untreated lemon	
1 small bunch parsley	

Preparation time: 20 minutes
Cooking time: 10-15 minutes
Nutritional value:

Analysis per serving, approx:
• 2155kJ/515kcal
• 49g protein
• 32g fat
• 2g carbohydrate

Gut and clean the trout carefully under running water, taking care not to damage the layer of mucous over the scales, which will produce the blue tint. Dry the inside of the fish and rub it with salt. Curl the fish up by using a trussing needle to pass a loop of fine string through the lower jaw and tail fin. • Lay the fish in a shallow bowl. Heat the vinegar and pour it over the fish. Boil the water, wine and salt in a fish kettle or other large pan and place the fish in the liquid, over a low heat. Poach for 10-15 minutes depending on the size of fish. The fish is cooked when the dorsal fin can be pulled easily away from the body. • Melt the butter and keep it warm on a hotplate. Wash and dry the lemon and cut it into wedges. Wash and dry the parsley. • Serve the trout garnished with lemon, parsley and the melted butter. • Delicious with fried potatoes and a fresh green salad.

Pan-fried Trout
Illustrated above right

4 fresh trout	
Juice of 1 lemon or 2 tbsps vinegar	
1 tsp salt	
4 tbsps flour	
100g/4oz butter	
1 untreated lemon	
1 bunch parsley	

Preparation time: 15 minutes
Cooking time: 15 minutes
Nutritional value:

Analysis per serving, approx:
• 2005kJ/480kcal
• 50g protein
• 28g fat
• 8g carbohydrate

If necessary, scale and clean the fish, then wash them thoroughly inside and out under running water. Dry the trout on kitchen paper and marinate for 10 minutes in the lemon juice or vinegar. • Sprinkle with salt both inside and outside and toss in the flour. Heat the butter in one large pan or two small pans. Fry the trout on both sides for about 12 minutes or until golden brown. • Wash and dry the lemon and parsley. Cut the lemon into wedges. Garnish the trout with lemon wedges and parsley sprigs. • Delicious served with potatoes in parsley and a mixed salad.

Our Tip: You can refine this recipe by scattering some toasted almond flakes, dry-roasted in frying-pan to a golden brown, over the fish just before serving. Pan-frying is also suitable for powan and pollan, as well as small saltwater fish such as green herrings, lemon sole and plaice.

Tempting Ragoûts

Vegetable purées are a good way of binding a delicate sauce

Mussel Ragoût in Cream Sauce

Illustrated above right

1½kg/3lb 6oz fresh mussels
2 onions
1 parsley root
250ml/8fl oz white wine
125ml/4fl oz water
2 bay leaves
8 peppercorns
300g/10oz courgettes
40g/1¼oz butter
250ml/9fl oz single cream
Salt and freshly ground white pepper
1 bunch dill

Preparation time: 1 hour
Nutritional value:

Analysis per serving, approx:
• 2635kJ/630kcal
• 47g protein
• 35g fat
• 20g carbohydrate

Scrub the mussels thoroughly under running water until the water runs clear. Discard any open shells. Slice the onions into rings; wash and coarsely chop the parsley. • In a large pan, heat the water, wine, onion rings, parsley, bay leaves and peppercorns and bring to the boil. Place the mussels in the stock, cover and boil for 10 minutes, shaking the pan gently from time to time. • Strain the mussels and reserve the liquid; discard any shells that have remained closed. • Peel and dice the courgettes and boil for 10 minutes in the mussel stock, then strain. • Scoop the mussel flesh from the shells. • Heat the butter in a pan and add the courgette purée. Stir in the cream. Leave over a low heat for 5 minutes. • Heat the mussel flesh in this sauce but do not allow further cooking; season with salt and pepper. Chop the dill finely and stir it into the ragoût. • Serve with boiled long-grain rice and lettuce.

Shrimps in Dill Sauce

Illustrated above left

400g/14oz shrimps
2 ripe avocados
40g/1½oz butter
375ml/15fl oz vegetable stock
125ml/4fl oz dry white wine
1 egg yolk
4 tbsps cream
Pinch each of salt and sugar
2 tbsps finely chopped dill

Preparation time: 30 minutes
Nutritional value:

Analysis per serving, approx:
• 1965kJ/470kcal
• 20g protein
• 38g fat
• 6g carbohydrate

De-vein the shrimps, then rinse and drain them. Cut the avocados in half, remove the stones, scoop out the flesh and rub it through a sieve. • Heat the butter in a pan, add the avocado purée and stir in the stock. Pour in the wine and allow the sauce to boil briefly. • Heat the shrimps in the sauce, but do not boil. Beat the egg yolk with the cream and stir into the hot sauce; season with salt and sugar. Finally, stir in the chopped dill. • Serve the ragoût in vol-au-vent cases, or with a firm boiled rice.

Our Tip: If your shrimps are still in the shell, proceed as follows. Hold the head in the left hand, grip the tail between the thumb and forefinger of your right hand and twist. Once the tail is removed, the flesh can also be removed easily from the head. The shells may be used for making fish stock.

Pan-Fried Fish

A dish in which fresh haddock comes into its own

250g/8oz onions	
5oz butter	
200g/7oz mushrooms	
1 tsp sea salt	
2 tbsps lemon juice	
1 tbsp finely chopped fresh parsley	
1kg/2¼lbs floury potatoes	
1 tbsp dill seed	
1 tbsp vegetable stock granules	
500g/1lb 2oz haddock	
1 tomato	
1 tbsp finely chopped fresh dill	

Preparation time: 30 minutes
Cooking time: 20 minutes
Nutritional value:
Analysis per serving, approx:
- 1715kJ/410kcal
- 30g protein
- 11g fat
- 48g carbohydrate

Chop the onions coarsely and fry them in the butter until they turn transparent; remove them from the pan and set aside. • Wash and dry the mushrooms and slice them thinly. Cover and sweat them in the pan for 5 minutes with ½ tsp salt, 1 tbsp lemon juice and the parsley. Remove the mushrooms from the pan after this time. • Peel and wash the potatoes, slice paper-thin and arrange them in alternate layers with the onions. Scatter dill seed and stock granules over the potatoes as you do so. • Wash and dry the fish and sprinkle with the remaining lemon juice and salt. Divide the fish into four portions and place in the pan. Top with mushrooms. Pour 1 cupful of water into the pan, cover and cook over a medium heat for about 20 minutes. • Wash the tomatoes and cut into wedges. Sprinkle the pan with dill and garnish with tomato wedges.

Stuffed Green Herrings

An unusual suggestion for a piquant meal

4 green herrings	
3 tbsps lemon juice	
1½ tsps sea salt	
2 tbsps tomato purée	
250g/8oz onions	
250g/8oz leeks	
2 tbsps butter	
500g/1lb 2oz tomatoes	
100ml/3 fl oz cream	
2 tbsps finely chopped fresh dill	

Preparation time: 30 minutes
Cooking time: 30 minutes
Nutritional value:
Analysis per serving, approx:
- 2865kJ/685kcal
- 38g protein
- 51g fat
- 16g carbohydrate

Scale and clean the herrings, wash them thoroughly inside and out and dry them on kitchen paper. Sprinkle the fish inside and outside with 2 tbsps lemon juice and 1 tsp salt. Spread some tomato purée in the body cavity of the fish. • Chop half of the onions into rings and dice the remainder. Clean the leek, cut it in half along its length and then slice it into small strips across. Fry the diced onions and leek strips briefly in butter. • Heat the oven to 180°C/350°F/Gas Mark 4. Lightly grease a soufflé dish or baking tin with butter. • Stuff the fish with the fried vegetables and top with an even sprinkling of onion rings. Slice the tomatoes and lay them on top of the fish. Mix the cream with the remaining lemon juice and salt, and pour the mixture over the fish. • Cook for 30 minutes in the oven until tender. • Serve with a sprinkling of dill. • Potatoes in parsley and a green salad make good accompaniments.

Spring Plaice

Buy the freshest plaice you can find

Pan-fried Mackerel with Tomatoes

Fish and tomatoes make a harmonious combination

4 plaice
4 tbsps lemon juice
150g/5¹/₂oz streaky bacon, rind removed
2 onions
1 bunch each parsley and dill
¹/₂ tsp salt
1 tsp freshly ground white pepper
2 tbsps flour
1 untreated lemon

Preparation time: 1¹/₄ hours
Nutritional value:

Analysis per serving, approx:
- 2385kJ/570kcal
- 53g protein
- 35g fat
- 8g carbohydrate

Cut off the spiny side-fins, head and tail of the fish. Sprinkle with lemon juice and leave for 10 minutes. • Dice the bacon finely and cut the onion into rings. Wash, dry and chop the dill and parsley. • Fry the bacon in its own fat over a medium heat until brown; then set it aside. Fry the onion rings to a golden brown in the bacon fat; set them aside with the bacon. • Pat the plaice dry, sprinkle with salt and pepper and toss in the flour. Shake any loose flour from the fillets, and fry the plaice one by one in the bacon fat over a medium heat for 3 or 4 minutes either side; keep them hot on a dish when done. • Reheat the bacon and onions in the frying fat, stir in the parsley and dill, then sprinkle over the plaice. • Wash and dry the lemon and cut into wedges to use as a garnish. • Excellent with a spicy potato salad.

1kg/2¹/₄lbs mackerel
2 tbsps lemon juice
2 pinches freshly ground white pepper
2 tbsps finely chopped fresh tarragon or 1 tbsp dried tarragon
1kg/2¹/₄lbs tomatoes
3 cloves garlic
1 tbsp olive oil
1 tsp sea salt
2 tsps finely chopped fresh basil or 1 tbsp dried basil
1 tbsp cracked wheat
125ml/4fl oz dry white wine

Preparation time: 40 minutes
Nutritional value:

Analysis per serving, approx:
- 2360kJ/565kcal
- 50g protein
- 32g fat
- 13g carbohydrate

Wash the mackerel and remove the heads. Slit the fish open lengthways, free the backbone and make a number of diagonal cuts in the skin. Sprinkle both sides of the fish with lemon juice and 1 tsp pepper. Push tarragon sprigs into the cuts in the skin and through the skin itself. • Skin the tomatoes by first making a cross-shaped cut in the skin, then plunging them into boiling water; chop them into quarters. Chop the garlic cloves very finely. • Heat the olive oil in a large pan. Fry the garlic until transparent, then add the tomatoes, the rest of the pepper, ¹/₂ tsp of salt and the basil. Bring to the boil rapidly once. • Mix the flour with the wine and pour over the tomatoes. • Lay the mackerel with their skins uppermost on the bed of tomatoes. Cover and cook over a medium heat for 10 - 15 minutes. • Season the fish and tomatoes with the remaining salt. • Goes well with potatoes with dill or parsley.

Saltwater Fish Plainly Cooked

Dishes that bring out the true flavour of saltwater fish

Haddock with Melted Butter
Illustrated above left

1kg/2¼ lbs sea fish trimmings
1 onion
1 carrot
1 leek
1 small bay leaf
1l/1¾ pints water
Salt and freshly ground white pepper
1 fresh haddock, ready to cook
1 untreated lemon
4 tarragon sprigs
125g/5oz butter

Preparation time: 40 minutes
Cooking time: 30 minutes
Nutritional value:
Analysis per serving, approx:
• 1880kJ/450kcal
• 46g protein
• 26g fat
• 6g carbohydrate

Wash the fish trimmings. Clean the onion, leek and carrot and cut them into chunks. Simmer the vegetables with the fish trimmings in the water for 30 minutes to make a fish fumet. • Strain the fumet and season with salt and pepper. Wash the haddock and place it in the fumet over a gentle heat for 25-30 minutes. • Remove the fish and slice it into four pieces, removing all bones as you do so. Wash and dry the lemon, and cut into wedges. Wash and dry the tarragon. Arrange the fish on a dish, garnished with lemon and tarragon. • Melt, but do not brown the butter. Sprinkle a little of the melted butter over the fish and serve the rest in a sauce boat. • Excellent with new potatoes.

Cod in Wine Sauce
Illustrated above right

4 cod steaks, weighing 200g/7oz each
Juice of half a lemon
½ tsp salt
2 carrots
1 bunch parsley
4 stalks celery
1 bay leaf
500ml/16fl oz dry white wine
Freshly ground white pepper
125ml/4fl oz crème fraîche
Some basil leaves

Preparation time: 40 minutes
Nutritional value:
Analysis per serving, approx:
• 1965kJ/470kcal
• 40g protein
• 26g fat
• 6g carbohydrate

Wash and dry the cod steaks, sprinkle with lemon juice and salt. Wash and skin the carrot, wash the parsley and the celery. Cut the celery into julienne strips. Place the prepared vegetables in a pan with the bay leaf and white wine, bring to the boil and simmer for about 5 minutes. Season this wine court-bouillon with pepper and stir in the crème fraîche. Discard the bunch of parsley • Poach the steaks in the sauce over a very low heat for about 10 minutes. • Garnish the steaks with basil. • Delicious with potatoes in parsley.

Our Tip: To feed a hungry crowd, add 300g/10oz frozen peas to the vegetable julienne and cook in the white wine for 5 minutes.

Fish and Vegetable Bakes

A most attractive way of serving fish

Cauliflower and Fish Bake
Illustrated above left

1 cauliflower
150g/5½oz millet
500ml/16fl oz water
1 tsp five-spice powder
1 tsp garlic salt
600g/1lb 6oz cod fillet
2 tbsps lemon juice
3 tbsps soy sauce
2 tbsps finely chopped fresh parsley
2 eggs
200ml/6fl oz cream
50g/2oz butter

Preparation time: 40 minutes
Cooking time: 20 minutes
Nutritional value:

Analysis per serving, approx:
• 2530kJ/605kcal
• 41g protein
• 31g fat
• 39g carbohydrate

Clean the cauliflower in lukewarm water and break it into florets. Cook in water for about 15 minutes with the millet, garlic salt and five-spice powder until tender. • Remove the pan from the heat and leave the millet to swell for a further 5 minutes. Strain the vegetables and millet through a sieve. • Wash and dry the fish and cut it into cubes. Mix the lemon juice, soy sauce and parsley in a bowl. Marinate the fish in this mixture. • Heat the oven to 200°C/400°F/Gas Mark 6. Grease a soufflé dish. • Separate the eggs. Combine the vegetables, marinated fish, egg yolks and cream. Beat the egg whites until they stand in stiff peaks, then carefully fold them into the fish and vegetable mixture. Fill the dish, dot with flakes of butter and bake for 20 minutes.

Redfish and Tomato Bake
Illustrated above right

800g/1lb 12oz redfish fillets
4 tbsps lemon juice
1kg/1¼lbs tomatoes
½ tsp salt
Freshly ground white pepper
1 onion
1-2 cloves of garlic
4 tbsps oil
1 bunch of thyme or ½ tsp dried thyme
1 bunch basil

Preparation time: 20 minutes
Cooking time: 30 minutes
Nutritional value:

Analysis per serving, approx:
• 1590kJ/380kcal
• 40g protein
• 20g fat
• 12g carbohydrate

Wash and dry the fish, then cut it into 3cm/1-inch strips; sprinkle it with lemon juice and leave to soak for 10 minutes. • Wash and slice the tomatoes, removing the hard knot where the stalk joins the fruit. • Heat the oven to 200°C/400°F/Gas Mark 6. Butter a soufflé dish. • Arrange the strips of fish and tomato slices in alternate bands across the dish; sprinkle with salt and pepper. • Chop the garlic and onion very finely and fry in butter until transparent. Wash the fresh thyme and stir the leaves into the onion and garlic. If you are using dried thyme, just rub it and scatter it over the pan. Top the tomatoes and fish with the onion mixture and cover the soufflé dish with a lid or aluminium foil. Bake on the middle shelf of the oven for 30 minutes. • Serve with a sprinkling of basil leaves cut into fine strips. • Delicious with mashed potatoes or rice.

Exquisitely Prepared Sea Fish

Popular and easily-digested dishes

Stuffed Rolled Sole

Illustrated above left

10 fillets of sole, weighing 100g/4oz each

250g/8oz fish trimmings

1 onion

200g/7oz mushrooms

50g/2oz butter

12 white peppercorns

¹/₂ bay leaf

375ml/15fl oz white wine

¹/₂ tsp each salt and white pepper

¹/₂ egg white plus 2 egg yolks

125ml/4fl oz cream

40g/1 ¹/₄ oz goose liver paté

2 shallots • 3 tbsps dry vermouth

Preparation time: 1¹/₂ hours
Nutritional value:
Analysis per serving, approx:
• 2425kJ/580kcal • 48g protein
• 27g fat • 8g carbohydrate

Wash and dry or drain the fish and fish trimmings. Cut the onion into rings. Wash the mushrooms and remove the stems, then slice the caps. • Melt 25g/1oz of the butter and fry the fish trimmings and onions. Add the mushroom stems, peppercorns, bay leaf and wine, cover and simmer for 30 minutes. • Cut two fillets into small pieces, season with salt and pepper and purée in a food processor. Mix in the ¹/₂ egg white and then the cream; process this mixture. Mix the liver paté into the stuffing and spread on the skin side of the remaining eight fillets. Roll up the fillets from their thick end and secure with wooden cocktail sticks. • Chop the shallots finely and fry in the remaining butter. Put the sliced mushrooms into the pan, followed by the rolled fillets. Add the strained fish stock, cover and sweat for 8 minutes. • Beat the egg yolks and the vermouth in a water bath until creamy. Keep the rolled fillets warm on a dish. Reduce the fish stock to a thick consistency, mix with the egg yolk and cream mixture and pour over the fish rolls. • Tasty with marrow balls braised in butter.

Sea Fish on a Bed of Vegetables

Illustrated above right

2 bunches of pot herbs (carrot, leek, turnip)

200g/7oz mushrooms

30g/1oz butter

1 small saltwater fish with head removed (haddock, ling or cod), about 1kg/2¹/₄lbs

3 tbsps lemon juice

Pinch white pepper

100ml/3fl oz cream

1 tbsp soya sauce

1 tsp each sea salt, dried thyme and paprika

2 tsps wholewheat flour

125ml/4fl oz white wine

200g/7oz shelled green peas

1 tsp each finely chopped fresh dill, parsley and basil

Preparation time: 45 minutes
Nutritional value:
Analysis per serving, approx:
• 1695kJ/405kcal • 50g protein
• 15g fat • 12g carbohydrate

Wash and finely chop the pot herbs. Thinly slice the mushrooms. • Melt the butter. Add the vegetables, cover the pan and sweat them for 5 minutes. • Wash the fish thoroughly, scaling and cleaning if necessary. Dry the fish well, sprinkle both inside and outside with 2 tbsps lemon juice and season with pepper. • Combine the cream, soya sauce, herbs, flour and wine and add to the vegetables, together with the peas. Lay the fish on top and cook over a gentle heat for about 20 minutes. • Season the vegetables with the remaining lemon juice and spices.

Fish and Mussel Stew

A light dish, high in protein

Norwegian Fish Mould

An unusual but delicious dish

500g/1lb 2oz fish trimmings
1 parsley sprig
1 untreated lemon
2 onions
4 celery stalks
4 allspice grains
750g/1lb 10oz mussels
1 clove garlic
2 tbsps butter
500ml/16fl oz dry white wine
400g/14oz cod or redfish fillets
½ tsp salt
1 tbsp finely chopped fresh dill

Preparation time: 1 hour
Nutritional value:
Analysis per serving, approx:
• 1715kJ/410kcal
• 41g protein
• 11g fat
• 16g carbohydrate

First make a fish fumet. Wash the fish trimmings, parsley and lemon. Slice the lemon. Peel the onion and celeriac. Dice the celery, then cook all the prepared ingredients together with the allspice over medium heat, in a covered pan, for 30 minutes. • Thoroughly scrub the mussels under running water; discard any open shells as you do so. Finely chop the second onion and the garlic and fry in the butter. Add the mussels and the wine, cover and cook for 15 minutes; shake the pan from time to time. • Strain the mussel stock and scoop the mussel flesh out of the shells; discard any mussels that have remained closed. • Strain the fumet and mix it with the mussel stock. Cut the fish into cubes, sprinkle with salt and leave in the stock over a gentle heat for 10 minutes. • Put the mussels into the stock to reheat. • Season the stew with salt and serve with a sprinkling of dill.

750g/1lb 10oz cod or redfish
1 day-old bread roll
250ml/4fl oz milk
40g/1¼oz streaky bacon
1 onion
3 eggs
1 tbsp cornflour
Pinch each salt and freshly grated nutmeg

Preparation time: 30 minutes
Cooking time: 1 hour
Nutritional value:
Analysis per serving, approx:
• 1965kJ/470kcal
• 45g protein
• 25g fat
• 16g carbohydrate

Wash and dry the fish, then cut it into coarse cubes. Soften the bread roll in 125ml/4 fl oz milk. Dice the bacon and finely chop the onion. • Fry half the bacon in its own fat in a pan. Sweat the onion in the bacon fat until it turns yellow, then set aside to cool. • Put the fish cubes, diced bacon, fried bacon and onion mixture through a mincer. Mix to a stiff paste with the eggs, the remaining milk, the cornflour and the bread roll, lightly squeezed out; season with salt and nutmeg. • Grease a jelly mould and sprinkle with breadcrumbs. Fill with the fish mixture and cover tightly. Place the mould in a water bath over a gentle heat for 1 hour. Take care that the water reaches no higher than about 3cm/1 inch below the edge of the pudding mould. • Remove the mould from the water. Leave to stand for a few minutes, then turn out and serve immediately. • Tastes excellent with a spicy tomato or herb sauce.

Waterzooi

This Belgian recipe can be adapted for poultry as well as fish

250g/8oz sea fish
1 large onion
1 bunch parsley
1 bay leaf
8 peppercorns
6 allspice grains
250ml/8fl oz dry white wine
Juice of 2 lemons
Salt
1 head celery
1 leek
2 carrots
25g/1oz butter
2 egg yolks
125ml/4fl oz cream
Freshly ground nutmeg

Preparation time: 1 hour
Nutritional value:
Analysis per serving, approx:
• 2340kJ/560kcal
• 62g protein
• 22g fat
• 17g carbohydrate

Wash the fish thoroughly, cut off heads and tails and remove bones. Place the fish trimmings in a large pan. Chop the onion into quarters. Wash the parsley and add it to the fish trimmings, together with the bay leaf, onion, peppercorns and allspice. Pour the wine over this and top up with water until the fish scraps are just covered. Simmer the liquid over a gentle heat for 30 minutes. • Chop the cleaned fish into chunks, sprinkle with lemon juice and salt. • Clean and slice the celery, leek and carrots. • Heat the butter in a large pan and sweat the vegetables for 5 minutes. Place the fish chunks on top, strain the liquid and pour 250ml/4 fl oz of it over the fish. Cover the fish and simmer for 15 minutes. • Beat the egg yolks and cream. Boil the remaining liquid vigorously for several minutes, then stir 2 tbsps into the egg and cream mixture. Remove the liquid from the stove and thicken with the cream; season with salt and nutmeg. • Pour the sauce over the cooked fish.

Jansson's Temptation

This Swedish dish requires fresh anchovies which are actually young Baltic herrings

750g/1lb10oz potatoes
20 tinned Swedish anchovies or pilchards
400g/14oz onions
40g/1¼oz butter
½ tsp freshly ground white pepper
200ml/6fl oz single cream
2 tbsps breadcrumbs
15g/½oz butter
Butter for the dish

Preparation time: 20 minutes
Cooking time: 1 hour
Nutritional value:

Analysis per serving, approx:
- 1880kJ/450kcal
- 7g protein
- 27g fat
- 43g carbohydrate

Wash and peel the potatoes; cut them first into slices, then into strips. Dry on kitchen paper. • Drain the tinned fish. Slice the onions thinly and fry in butter until transparent, then set aside to cool.

• Heat the oven to 220°C/ 400°F/Gas Mark 6. Butter a flameproof dish. • Place half of the potatoes in the dish and sprinkle with pepper. Arrange anchovy fillets and onion rings on top of the potatoes, then top with a layer of the remaining potatoes. Pour the cream over the potatoes, sprinkle with pepper and breadcrumbs. Finally dot with flaked butter. • Cover the dish with aluminium foil and bake on the middle shelf for 30 minutes. • Remove the foil and bake for a further 30 minutes, until a golden crust forms. • Delicious with a fresh salad.

Matelote

A French seafarer's dish made with white wine

For 6 servings:
1 kg/2¼ lbs mixed freshwater fish, e.g. eel, perch, trout, tench
1½ tsps salt
½ tsp black pepper
2 onions
2 shallots
250g/8oz mushrooms
100g/4oz butter
2 tbsps cognac
500ml/16fl oz dry white wine
1 bouquet garni, consisting of 1 bay leaf, 6 parsley sprigs and 1 fresh thyme sprig
Juice of 1 lemon
100ml/3fl oz crème fraîche
1 tbsp flour
200g/7oz tagliatelle
1 tsp salt

Preparation time: 40 minutes
Nutritional value:

Analysis per serving, approx:
- 2925kJ/700kcal
- 36g protein
- 40g fat
- 33g carbohydrate

Wash the fish thoroughly, pat dry and cut into portions; season with salt and pepper. Chop the onions and shallots. Wash the mushrooms and cut larger caps in half or quarters. • Fry the diced onions and shallots in 50g/2oz butter until they turn transparent, then add the fish and fry for 1 minute, stirring constantly. Pour the cognac over the fish, allow it to evaporate a little, then top up with wine and simmer for 5 minutes. • Add the mushrooms and bouquet garni to the fish, along with the lemon juice and crème fraîche; allow to simmer for 7 or 8 minutes. •Cream the remaining butter with the flour. • Cook the pasta in salted water until al dente. • Arrange the fish in a deep dish. Bind the sauce with the creamed flour and butter, cook for 3 minutes, season again and pour over the fish.

Mussel Risotto

Be ready to yearn for Mediterranean sun and sea

Fish Roulade

The right choice for a special occasion

1 onion	
1 clove garlic	
30g/2oz butter	
250g/8oz short-grain rice	
500ml/16fl oz chicken stock	
250ml/8fl oz dry white wine	
125-250ml/4-8fl oz hot water	
1 bay leaf	
2 dried chilli peppers	
250g/8oz freshly cooked shelled mussels (from about 1½kg/3lb 6oz mussels in the shell) or canned mussels	
50g/2oz freshly grated Parmesan cheese	
Salt and freshly ground black pepper	
Some fresh basil leaves	

Preparation time: 50 minutes
Nutritional value:
Analysis per serving, approx:
* 1985kJ/475kcal
* 17g protein
* 18g fat
* 55g carbohydrate

Chop the onion and garlic finely. Heat the butter in a pan and fry the onion and garlic until they turn a golden yellow. Add the rice and fry, stirring constantly, then add the stock, wine and water. Add the bay leaf and chillies. Bring to the boil, then leave the rice over a gentle heat for 30 to 40 minutes. • Drain the mussels and stir into the rice 5 minutes or so before the rice is cooked. Remove the bay leaf and chillies. Stir the cheese into the rice. Season well with salt and pepper. Wash the basil, cut it into strips and scatter it over the risotto. • Excellent with a mixed salad and the same white wine used in the dish itself.

800g/1lb 12oz Savoy cabbage	
1 tsp salt	
4 redfish fillets, 200g/7oz each	
Juice of half a lemon	
4 tbsps crème fraîche	
2 eggs	
½ tsp freshly ground white pepper	
2 tbsps mustard	
½ tsp dried basil	
2 tbsps sesame oil	
125ml/4fl oz white wine	
125ml/4fl oz vegetable stock	

Preparation time: 40 minutes
Cooking time: 30 minutes
Nutritional value:
Analysis per serving, approx:
* 1800kJ/430kcal
* 45g protein
* 20g fat
* 10g carbohydrate

Clean the cabbage and blanch in boiling salted water for 8 to 10 minutes. • Wash and dry the fillets and chop them coarsely; purée them in a food processor with the lemon juice, crème fraîche, eggs, pepper and 1 tbsp mustard. Rub the basil and mix it into the fish stuffing and season with salt. • Pull 12 to 16 of the outer leaves off the cabbage. Pare down the heavy central stalks. Lay three or four leaves over one another and top with the fish stuffing. Fold the leaves from the side and finally roll up the roulades; secure with fine string and fry all over in 1 tbsp oil. Mix the remaining mustard with the white wine and pour over the roulades. Cover and braise the roulades for 30 minutes. • Chop the rest of the cabbage finely and cook in the remaining oil, with added vegetable stock, for 15 minutes. Season the cabbage with salt and pepper then arrange it with the roulades.

Clam Chowder

An American version of a satisfying mussel soup

500g/1lb 2oz frozen clams or 200g/7oz canned mussels in brine
500g/1lb 2oz potatoes
1 large onion
50g/2oz streaky bacon
25g/1oz butter
1 tbsp flour
375ml/15fl oz hot milk
About 250ml/5fl oz hot water
125ml/4fl oz cream
1 tbsp finely chopped fresh parsley
Salt and freshly ground black pepper

Preparation time: 1 hour
Nutritional value:
Analysis per serving, approx:
- 1985kJ/475kcal
- 23g protein
- 26g fat
- 37g carbohydrate

Thoroughly wash the frozen mussels and boil them in a covered pot with 250ml/8fl oz of water over a high flame for 3-5 minutes until the shells open. Shake the pan from time to time. Remove any mussels that do not open. • Strain the mussel stock through a fine sieve. Drain the canned mussels as necessary, but reserve the liquid. • Peel and dice the potatoes and cook in a little water for 10 minutes. • Finely dice the onion and slice the bacon into strips; fry them in butter. Stir in the flour and fry until it turns bright yellow; gradually add the milk and mussel liquid. Top up with water. Allow to boil for 5 minutes. • Strain the potatoes, purée half of them and then stir, with the diced potatoes, back into the soup. Heat briefly. Add the cream and parsley and season with salt and pepper.

Bouillabaisse

This is just one version of Europe's best-known fish soup

To serve 8:

800g/1lb 12oz firm-fleshed fish such as turbot, halibut, sole and lamprey, ready to cook

800g/1lb 12oz soft-fleshed fish such as cod, haddock, whiting and red mullet

750g/1lb 10oz fish bones and trimmings, such as heads and fins

3 small leeks

3 onions

3 cloves garlic

1 tsp each finely chopped fresh thyme, oregano and savory

Pinch of saffron

125ml/4fl oz olive oil

1 bay leaf

1¹/₂ tsps salt

2-3 tsps freshly ground white pepper

1l/1³/₄ pints water

3 large beefsteak tomatoes

Preparation time: 1¹/₂ hours
Nutritional value:

Analysis per serving, approx:
- 1465kJ/350kcal
- 38g protein
- 18g fat
- 8g carbohydrate

Thoroughly wash all the fish, bones and trimmings in cold water. Dry the fish pieces and drain the trimmings. • Cut the leeks in half along their length, cut off the root end and the dark green upper leaves, wash thoroughly, spin dry, and cut into fine strips. Wash the dark green leaves, cut them into strips and set them aside. Chop the onion and garlic very finely, keeping them separate from one another. • Cover and marinate the firm and the soft fish separately, each in a mixture of half the garlic, herbs, saffron and 3 tbsps oil. • Boil the fish bones and trimmings in a covered pan for 35 minutes together with the dark green leek strips, a chopped onion, the bay leaf and the salt and pepper. •

Heat the remaining oil and fry the rest of the onion and the lighter leek strips for 3 minutes. Add the firm-fleshed fish with its marinade, strain the fish stock into the pan and boil gently for 5 minutes. • Skin the tomatoes by cutting a cross in top and bottom and plunging them into boiling water. Cut them in half, remove the hard knot where the stalk joins the fruit and dice them coarsely. • Add the soft-fleshed fish, tomatoes and marinade to the pan and cook gently for a further 8 minutes. • Season the bouillabaisse well with salt and pepper. • Tastes excellent with thin slices of white bread that have been baked briefly in the oven, and spread with garlic butter if desired.

Our Tip: From one fishing village to the next there is a vast range of variations on the bouillabaisse theme. In some homes you will find potatoes in it, while in another shrimps or

mussels make an appearance. In gastronomic circles they swear by a strip of dried orange peel as an additional flavouring. So the individual can experiment to find a favourite combination. Bouillabaisse can be eaten like a stew, or else the fish may be served alone, leaving the tasty broth to be sampled separately, as desired.

Stuffed Catfish

A saltwater fish of excellent quality

1 catfish, weighing 1½kg/3lb 6oz

Juice of 1 lemon

½ tsp white pepper

200g/7oz mushrooms

2 shallots

½ tsp salt

200ml/6fl oz crème fraîche

Pinch of white pepper

200g/7oz white bread

1 bunch of chervil

1 egg

Pinch of grated nutmeg

Preparation time: 40 minutes
Cooking time: 35 minutes
Nutritional value:

Analysis per serving, approx:
- 2740kJ/655kcal
- 35g protein
- 45g fat
- 17g carbohydrate

Scale and clean the fish, wash it thoroughly in cold water and pat dry. Remove the fins and gills. Sprinkle the fish inside and out with lemon juice; rub salt into the body cavity. • Clean the mushrooms and chop them finely, then squeeze them out in a kitchen towel: the mushroom juice is not required. Finely chop the shallots, add them to a pan containing the mushrooms, salt and 2 tbsps crème fraîche and reduce, stirring constantly. Cut the crusts off the bread, cut it into cubes and then process in a food processor with the chervil. • Heat the oven to 200°C/400°F/Gas Mark 6. Smear a baking pan with plenty of butter. Mix the cooled mushrooms with the bread, egg and nutmeg. Stuff the fish and secure the body cavity opening with a wooden cocktail stick or fine string. • Lay the catfish in the pan and bake for about 35 minutes on the lowest shelf of the oven. •During the last 15 minutes in the oven, spread beaten crème fraîche over the fish. • Gherkins or cucumber with dill and fried potatoes go well with this.

Baked Redfish

Juicy foil-baked fish from the oven

1 redfish, cleaned, weighing about 1½kg/3lb 6oz

4 tbsps lemon juice

3 slices bread

3 cloves garlic

1 bunch parsley

1 tsp salt

Pinch of freshly ground white pepper

1 tbsp paprika

6 tbsps olive oil

1 untreated lemon

Preparation time: 20 minutes
Baking time: 40 minutes
Nutritional value:

Analysis per serving, approx:
- 1630kJ/390kcal
- 45g protein
- 19g fat
- 6g carbohydrate

Cut the fins off the fish and scale it, starting at the tail. Wash it inside and out, dry it and sprinkle all over with lemon juice.

• Remove the crusts from the bread and crumble into fine crumbs. Chop the garlic finely. Wash the parsley, shake it dry, then chop finely and mix with the garlic. • Heat the oven to 200°C/400°F/Gas Mark 6. Rub the fish inside and out with the salt and pepper. Spread half of the parsley and garlic mixture in the body cavity. Lay the fish on the foil. Mix together the rest of the parsley, the bread, the paprika and the oil and spread the mixture over the fish. • Bake the redfish for 40 minutes on the middle shelf. • Wash and dry the lemon and cut into wedges. Serve with a lemon garnish. • Delicious with fried potatoes seasoned with thyme and bay leaf, and a fresh green salad.

Fish au Gratin

The tasty crust also protects the fish

500ml/16fl oz water	
2 tsps vegetable stock granules	
200g/7oz coarse oatmeal	
4 onions	
200g/7oz mushrooms	
500g/1lb 2oz carrots	
100g/4oz butter	
3 tbsps finely chopped fresh parsley • 1 tsp sea salt	
$^1\!/_2$ tsp white pepper	
500g/1lb 2oz coley or hake fillet	
1 tbsp lemon juice	
200g/7oz Cheddar cheese	

Preparation time: 1 hour
Nutritional value:
Analysis per serving, approx:
• 2720kJ/650kcal
• 60g protein
• 40g fat
• 2g carbohydrate

Boil the water with the stock in a small saucepan, stir in the oatmeal, cover and cook over a low flame for 10 minutes. •

Remove the pan from the heat and allow the oatmeal to swell for a further 10 minutes. • Dice the onions. Clean and chop the carrots and mushrooms. Fry the diced onions in 50g/2oz butter until they turn transparent. Add the carrots, mushrooms, half the parsley and some salt and pepper and sweat for 5 minutes. • Sprinkle the fish with the lemon juice, salt and pepper, lay it on top of the vegetables and sweat for a further 8 minutes. • Grate the cheese coarsely. Grease a flameproof dish and heat the oven to 240°C/450°F/Gas Mark 8. • Mix the oatmeal with one third of the vegetables and spread a layer over the base of the dish. Arrange the fish in chunks over the top. Mix the rest of the vegetables with the cheese and cover the fish with the mixture. Dot with the remaining butter. • Bake for 10 minutes on the top shelf of the oven. Sprinkle with the remaining parsley. • Eat with a green salad.

Chinese Fish and Rice

Lovers of spicy food should try this

1 large onion	
400g/14oz fennel	
1 red pepper	
3 tbsps sesame oil	
150g/5 $^1\!/_2$oz brown rice	
250ml/8fl oz water	
2 tbsps soya sauce	
500g/1lb 2oz redfish fillet	
1 tbsp lemon juice	
250g/8oz sharp apples	
100g/4oz shrimps	
50g/2oz raisins	
150g/5$^1\!/_2$oz bean sprouts	
1 tsp dried dill	

Preparation time: 1 hour
Nutritional value:
Analysis per serving, approx:
• 1465kJ/350kcal
• 14g protein
• 9g fat
• 55g carbohydrate

Dice the onion; wash the pepper and fennel then cut them into fine strips. Fry the onion

until transparent in the oil. Add and fry the rice. Stir-fry the fennel and pepper over a gentle heat for 10 minutes with the onion and rice. Add the water and soya sauce and simmer for 25 minutes. • Cut up the fish and sprinkle with lemon juice. Chop the apple into quarters, peel it and remove the core, then slice thinly. Put the fish chunks and apple in the pan and leave for 10 minutes. • If necessary, remove the shrimps' intestines, then wash and drain them. Wash the raisins in hot water, drain them, then put them in the pan with the bean sprouts, shrimps and dill. Gently mix all the ingredients together, season with more salt if necessary and heat through.

Arabian-style Perch

Surprise your guests with this Middle Eastern dish

To serve 6:

1 perch weighing about 1¹/₂kg/3lb 6oz
3 tsps salt
150ml/8fl oz olive oil
3 onions
1 green pepper
50g/2oz shelled walnuts
3 tbsps finely chopped fresh parsley
3 tbsps pomegranate seeds or 200g/7oz grapes
¹/₂ tsp black pepper
3 cloves garlic
100g/4oz tahini
4 tbsps lemon juice

Preparation time: 30 minutes
Cooking time: 50 minutes
Nutritional value:
Analysis per serving, approx:
• 2415kJ/575kcal
• 51g protein
• 36g fat
• 9g carbohydrate

Wash the fish thoroughly, pat it dry and rub with 1 tsp of the salt. Grease a flameproof dish with half the oil. Toss the fish in the oil and leave to marinate for 15 minutes. • Heat the oven to 200°C/400°F/Gas Mark 6. • For the stuffing, dice the onions finely, remove the stalk and seeds from the pepper, then wash, dry and dice it. Take 2 tbsps of oil from the dish and heat in a pan. Fry the pepper and onion over high heat. • Chop the walnuts coarsely and add to the vegetables; fry for a further 5 minutes. Stir in 2 tbsps chopped parsley and a similar amount of pomegranate seeds, or 100g/4oz seeded grapes; season with 1 tsp salt and the pepper. • Stuff the perch and secure the opening in the body with a wooden cocktail stick. Bake the fish for about 50 minutes. • Crush the garlic and mix with the tahini, the remaining olive oil, 4 tbsps water, the lemon juice and the remaining salt. • Sprinkle the fish with the remaining pomegranate seeds and parsley. • Serve with the sesame sauce and rice.

Coley with Tomatoes

A common fish in an unusual combination

To serve 6:

1½kg/3lb 6oz coley
1 tbsp lemon juice
1 onion
8 tomatoes
1 large potato
Salt and white pepper
2 tbsps oil
50g/2oz fat bacon, thinly sliced
250ml/9fl oz meat or vegetable stock
½ tsp dried basil
250ml/9fl oz sour cream
Some fresh basil leaves

Preparation time: 40 minutes
Cooking time: about 40 minutes
Nutritional value:

Analysis per serving, approx:
• 1655kJ/395kcal
• 50g protein
• 17g fat
• 10g carbohydrate

Wash the fish inside and out under cold running water; dry on kitchen paper. In each flank of the fish, make two cuts, reaching almost to the backbone, then rub the fish with lemon juice. • Slice the onion into fine rings. Skin the tomatoes by cutting a cross in the skin top and bottom, then immersing them in boiling water for about 2 minutes. Cut the skinned tomatoes into quarters and remove the hard knot where the stalk joins the fruit. • Heat the oven to 200°C/400°F/Gas Mark 6. • Peel and wash the potatoes. • Dry the fish and rub the inside with salt. • Heat the oil in a large pan and fry the onion rings until transparent, turning constantly. • Push the potato into the body cavity of the fish and place it in the pan; the potato will help to balance the fish so that it does not fall over in the pan. • Cover the fish with slices of bacon. Bake the coley on the bottom shelf of the oven for about 40 minutes. • Heat

the meat or vegetable stock. Pour half of it around the fish after 10 minutes in the oven. Surround the fish with the tomatoes. Gradually add the rest of the stock as baking progresses. • Remove the bacon rashers after 25 minutes. Add the dried basil to the sour cream. Pour this over the fish and bake for another 10 to 15 minutes. The fish should end up a crisp, golden brown. • Dice the bacon rashers. Wash and dry the basil, then cut into thin strips. • Arrange the baked fish on a heated serving dish. Spoon the sauce out of the pan with the onion rings and tomatoes, seasoning with salt and freshly ground white pepper to taste. Top with a scattering of bacon and basil strips. • Delicious with fried potatoes or mashed potatoes and a pea and sweetcorn salad.

Our Tip: Cod can also be prepared in this way. Instead of the bed of onions, bake the fish

over a bed of diced potato. Substitute the sour cream for a sprinkling of breadcrumbs mixed with finely chopped parsley and garlic, and dot with butter. Haddock is good baked on chopped mixed vegetables - carrots, leeks, peas and cauliflower for instance. Use a breadcrumb mixture in the same way as for cod.

Delicacies for Special Occasions

From trout to pike-perch, including pike, carp and salmon, here are feasts to serve hot or cold

Feasts of Sole

Both with vegetable accompaniments, but each a distinctive dish

Fried Sole with Fine Vegetables

Illustrated above left

250g/8oz young carrots
Pinch of salt
4 sole, weighing 300g/10oz each
3 tbsps lemon juice
750g/1lb10oz spinach
250g/8oz mushrooms
100g/4oz butter
¹/₂ tsp each of salt and freshly ground white pepper
2 tbsps flour
1 untreated lemon
Some parsley sprigs
2 tbsps finely chopped fresh parsley

Preparation time: 1¹/₄ hours
Nutritional value:

Analysis per serving, approx:
• 2340kJ/560kcal
• 62g protein
• 26g fat
• 19g carbohydrate

Scrape and wash the carrots, then cut them into julienne strips and sweat in a little salted water for 10 minutes. • Wash and dry the sole; sprinkle with 2 tbsps lemon juice and a little salt. • Wash the spinach thoroughly and leave it dripping wet; heat in the water and cook for 5 minutes or until wilted. • Wash the mushrooms and slice thinly, sprinkle with the remaining lemon juice and fry for 5 minutes in 20g/³/₄oz butter. • Strain the carrots and spinach and stir half the remaining butter into each of them. Season the vegetables with salt and pepper. • Dry the fish, dredge lightly with flour and fry on either side for 8-10 minutes until golden brown. Keep the cooked sole warm. • Arrange the fish on a heated dish and garnish with parsley and slices of lemon. Scatter chopped parsley over the vegetables.

Fillets of Fish 'Tre Verde'

Illustrated above right

150g/5¹/₂oz leeks
250g/8oz courgettes
250g/8oz asparagus
30g/1oz butter
150g/5 ¹/₂oz shelled green peas
Pinch of garlic salt
500g/1lb 2oz small sole or plaice fillets
2 tbsps lemon juice
¹/₂ tsp each of sea salt and freshly ground white pepper
1 tbsp finely chopped fresh dill
1-2 untreated lemons

Preparation time: 25 minutes
Nutritional value:

Analysis per serving, approx:
• 965kJ/230kcal
• 27g protein
• 8g fat
• 13g carbohydrate

Wash the leeks, courgettes and asparagus. Cut the leeks into fine strips, the courgettes into thin slices and the asparagus into pieces 4-5cm/1¹/₂-2 inches long. • Melt 20g/³/₄oz butter in a large pan. First fry the leek, then the courgettes and then the asparagus in the butter. Finally add the peas and 125ml/4 fl oz water. Scatter the garlic salt over the vegetables and sweat over a gentle heat for 10 minutes. • Wash and dry the fish, sprinkle with lemon juice and some salt and pepper. Lay the fish on top of the vegetables and leave to cook over a very low heat for 5-10 minutes, depending on the thickness of the fillets. • Dot the fish with the rest of the butter and sprinkle with dill. Garnish with lemon slices.

Foil-baked Halibut

The centrepiece of a dinner party

To serve 8:
250g/8oz shallots
2 each yellow, green and red peppers
500g/1lb 2oz tomatoes
1 leek
2 fresh green chillies
5 tbsps oil
1 tsp salt
2 pinches freshly ground white pepper
2kg/4¹/₂lbs halibut
¹/₂ bunch of parsley

Preparation time: 40 minutes
Cooking time: 50 minutes
Nutritional value:

Analysis per serving, approx:

- 1295kJ/310kcal
- 53g protein
- 6g fat
- 10g carbohydrate

Peel the shallots. Cut the peppers in half and remove the seeds; wash and cut into strips. Plunge the tomatoes in boiling water, skin them and cut them into quarters; remove the tough core where the stalk joins the fruit as you do so. Remove the dark green leaves from the leek. Wash the lighter, lower portion and slice into rings. Wash the green chillies, discard the seeds and dice finely. • Heat the oven to 200°C/400°F/Gas Mark 6. • Heat the oil in a large pan with a lid and fry the shallots until they turn bright yellow. Add the rest of the prepared vegetables, season with salt and pepper and sweat them for about 4 minutes. • Make an envelope out of a square of foil and fill it with half the vegetables. Set the remaining vegetables aside to keep hot. • Wash and dry the fish, rub with salt and pepper and place on the vegetables in the foil. Fold up the envelope to seal it and make several holes in the upper surface. Place the wrapped fish on the middle shelf of the oven. Bake for 50 minutes. • Fillet the fish, arrange it on a heated serving dish and surround it with vegetables. Wash and chop the parsley and scatter it over the dish.

Fine Fish in Tasty Bacon

Bacon gives a tang to delicate fish and protects it during baking

Catfish in Bacon
Illustrated above left

2 catfish, weighing
500g/1lb 2oz each

1 tbsp lemon juice

2 onions

4 green peppers

2 tbsps oil • 1 tsp salt

Pinch of white pepper

100g/4oz thin streaky bacon
rashers

500ml/16fl oz dry white wine

4 fully ripe beefsteak tomatoes

Preparation time: 20 minutes
Cooking time: 35 minutes
Nutritional value:
Analysis per serving, approx:
• 2445kJ/585kcal
• 44g protein
• 30g fat
• 15g carbohydrate

Wash and dry the fish both inside and out; make three diagonal cuts in each flank of the fish reaching almost to the depth of the backbone. Rub the catfish with lemon juice. • Cut the onion into rings. Cut the peppers in half and remove the seeds; wash and cut into strips. Heat the oven to 200°C/400°F/Gas Mark 6. •Heat the oil in a large pan. Fry the onions and strips of pepper. • Rub the inside of the fish with salt and pepper and lay it on the bed of vegetables. Arrange the bacon rashers in a fan shape on the fish and pour half the white wine over them. • Bake the fish on the lowest shelf of the oven for about 35 minutes. Gradually add the rest of the white wine as cooking progresses. • Skin the tomatoes by slitting the skin at one end and plunging them in boiling water; discard the tough core where the stalk joins the fruit. When the fish has been cooking for 25 minutes, add the tomatoes to it. • Delicious with mashed potatoes.

Trout in Bacon
Illustrated above right

4 ready-to-cook trout, weighing
200g/7oz each

Juice of 1 lemon

1 tsp salt

1 clove garlic

4 tsps finely chopped fresh dill

4 tsps finely chopped fresh
parsley

60g/2oz full-fat fromage frais

2 tbsps milk

100g/4oz thin streaky bacon
rashers

2 shallots

15g/¹/₂oz butter

125ml/4fl oz vegetable stock

4 dried rosemary sprigs

Preparation time: 15 minutes
Cooking time: 25 minutes
Nutritional value:
Analysis per serving, approx:
• 1925kJ/460kcal
• 43g protein
• 29g fat
• 3g carbohydrate

Heat the oven to 200°C/400°F/Gas Mark 6. • Wash the trout inside and out in cold water, dry, rub with lemon juice and season with salt. • Chop the garlic very finely. Mix with the dill, parsley, fromage frais and milk and coat the inside of the fish. Wrap the bacon around the fish and place them next to each other in a large flameproof dish. Bake in the oven for 25 minutes until tender. • Dice the shallots and fry them in the butter until transparent. In an open pan, gently boil the vegetable stock with the rosemary for 5 minutes. Pour this stock over the shallots; 10 minutes before the trout is ready, spoon the mixture over the fish. • Delicious with French bread and a green salad.

Variations on Scampi

You can never have too many scampi recipes

Chinese Deep-fried Scampi
Illustrated above left

16 peeled giant prawns
1/2 tsp salt
50g/2oz cornflour
1 egg white
125g/5oz carrots
150g/6oz shelled green peas
2 tbsps oil
250ml/9fl oz tomato ketchup
1 tbsp soya sauce
2 tbsps vinegar
2 tbsps sugar
1 tbsp cornflour
1l/1³/₄ pints of oil for frying

Preparation time: 40 minutes
Nutritional value:
Analysis per serving, approx:
• 3720kJ/890kcal
• 72g protein
• 50g fat
• 37g carbohydrate

De-vein the prawns. Wash and salt the prawns and toss them in cornflour. Toss the prawns in the lightly beaten egg white and then once more in cornflour. • Heat the oil to 175°C/350°F in the deep-fat fryer. Fry the scampi in portions for about 5 minutes or until golden brown. • Drain on kitchen paper and keep hot. Scrape and wash the carrots, then slice into fine julienne strips. Fry the carrots with the peas in oil. Add the ketchup, soya sauce, vinegar and sugar. Allow to cook for a few minutes. • Mix the cornflour with a little cold water and bind the sauce. • Serve the scampi with the sauce.

Flambéed Scampi
Illustrated above right

16 giant prawns in their shells
1 tsp coarse salt
30g/1oz butter
2 measures Pernod (2¹/₂ tbsps)
1 small clove garlic
250ml/8fl oz cream
Pinch of salt
1/2 tsp freshly ground white pepper
Pinch each of ground aniseed and sugar
1 tsp lemon juice
1/2 bunch spring onions
2 tomatoes

Preparation time: 45 minutes
Nutritional value:
Analysis per serving, approx:
• 2550kJ/610kcal
• 70g protein
• 32g fat
• 11g carbohydrate

Put the prawns in boiling salted water for 3 - 5 minutes. • Remove the shells and intestines. • Heat the butter in a pan and fry the prawns briefly. Pour in the Pernod, set it alight and allow it to burn out. Take the prawns out of the pan and set them aside. Crush the garlic into the frying fat. Thicken with cream and season with salt and pepper, aniseed, sugar and lemon juice. Cook until it acquires a creamy consistency. • Wash the spring onions and cut them into fine rings. Skin the tomatoes by plunging them in boiling water; chop them into quarters, remove the seeds and finally dice the flesh. Put the spring onions and tomatoes in the sauce and bring to the boil briefly. Reheat the scampi in the sauce but prevent further cooking. • Freshly crisped French bread and a fresh green salad with mixed herbs round the dish off perfectly.

Classic Carp Dishes

If you have difficulty choosing between these two, try the less well-known one

Carp Oriental Style
Illustrated above left

½ carp weighing about 800g/1lb12oz (cut lengthways)

1 bunch pot herbs (carrot, leek, turnip)

1 tbsp lemon juice

2 pinches freshly ground white pepper

2 tbsps rolled oats

4 shallots

2 tbsps sesame oil

250ml/8fl oz dry white wine

50g/2oz blanched almonds

1 tbsp raisins

250g/8oz white grapes

Pinch of ground clove

½ tsp sea salt

1 tbsp chive rings

½ tsp each finely chopped fresh or dried basil and marjoram

Preparation time: 50 minutes
Nutritional value:
Analysis per serving, approx:
- 2030kJ/485kcal • 40g protein
- 22g fat • 20g carbohydrate

Prepare a stock by boiling the head and fins of the carp for 15 minutes with the washed herbs; strain and measure out 125ml/4 fl oz of stock. • Sprinkle the fish with the lemon juice and pepper. • Roast the oatmeal in a dry pan, then remove and set aside. Cut the shallots into rings and fry in oil until transparent. Add the wine. Place the fish on top, cover, and cook for 10-15 minutes over a low heat. • Chop the almonds coarsely, wash the raisins in hot water, cut the grapes in half and remove the seeds. • Set the fish aside to keep hot. Put the oatmeal, almonds, raisins and grapes in the pan and add the fish stock. • Skin and bone the fish and cut into pieces. Add the herbs and seasonings.

Polish-style Carp
Illustrated above right

To serve 6:

1 carp, ready to cook, weighing about 1.8kg/4lbs

6 tbsps vinegar

50g/2oz raisins

1 bunch pot herbs (carrot, leek, turnip)

1 onion

30g/2oz butter

375ml/15fl oz warm water

1 bay leaf • ½ tsp salt

Pinch each of pepper and ground allspice

750ml/1 pint stout

50g/2oz ginger snaps

1 tbsp flour

½ tsp lemon juice

Pinch of sugar

Standing time: 30 minutes
Preparation time: 1¼ hours
Nutritional value:

Analysis per serving, approx:
- 2175kJ/520kcal • 56g protein
- 21g fat • 14g carbohydrate

Remove the head and tail of the fish. Cut the carp in half lengthways and cut each half into three portions. Wash thoroughly, sprinkle with vinegar and leave to stand for 30 minutes. • Wash the raisins and soften them in warm water. • Wash and chop the herbs. Dice the onion and fry for 5 -10 minutes in the butter. Pour in the water and seasonings and simmer for 15 minutes. • Add half the stout and leave to stand for 5 minutes. Soften the ginger snaps in the remaining stout, add to the vegetables and cook. • Squeeze the raisins dry and place them in the sauce with the pieces of carp; leave for 15-20 minutes. • Set the fish aside on a heated dish. • Mix the flour with a little cold water and thicken the sauce, season with salt and pepper, lemon juice and sugar.

Gilt Head Bream Roman Style

Gilt head bream is a great delicacy

| 4 gilt head bream, weighing about 300g/10oz each |
| Juice of 1 lemon |
| 2 onions |
| 1 head of lettuce |
| 1 tsp salt |
| $^1/_2$ tsp white pepper |
| 250ml/8fl oz dry white wine |
| 300g/10oz shelled green peas |
| 125ml/4fl oz cream |
| 50g/2oz butter |
| 2 tbsps milk |
| 2 tbsps finely chopped fresh dill |

Preparation time: $1^1/_4$ hours
Nutritional value:
Analysis per serving, approx:
• 2800kJ/670kcal • 63g protein
• 32g fat • 22g carbohydrate

Scale the bream, clean if necessary and wash thoroughly, inside and out. Dry the fish and sprinkle the inside with lemon juice. • Chop the onion finely and cut the lettuce into fine strips. • Heat the oven to 180°C/350°F/Gas Mark 4. Butter a baking tin and scatter the chopped onions over the base. Arrange the lettuce strips over the onions and sprinkle with salt and pepper. Lay the fish on top and sprinkle with 2 tbsps white wine. Cook for about 25 minutes on the bottom shelf of the oven until tender. • Arrange the fish on an ovenproof serving dish and leave it in the oven, with the heat turned off, to keep hot. • Transfer the onions, lettuce and juices from the baking tin to a saucepan. Add the remaining wine and the peas, cover and cook on gentle heat for 5 minutes. Reduce the mixture in the uncovered pan for 2 minutes. Add the cream and cook for 1 minute. Mix the flour and butter and stir into the sauce a little at a time; cook for 1 minute. Season the sauce with salt and pepper, pour it over the fish and garnish with dill. • A spinach pasta rounds the dish off perfectly.

Sea Bream Tuscan Style

This Mediterranean fish is a popular ingredient in Tuscan cuisine

| 2 sea bream, ready to cook, weighing about 500g/1lb 2oz each |
| Juice of 1 lemon |
| 1 large onion |
| 2 cloves garlic |
| 500g/1lb 2oz beefsteak tomatoes |
| 1 courgette |
| 4 tbsps olive oil |
| 250ml/8fl oz Tuscan white wine |
| $^1/_2$-1 tsp salt |
| Pinch of coarsely ground black pepper |
| 100g/4oz black olives |
| 1 bunch of basil |

Preparation time: 30 minutes
Baking time: 20 minutes
Nutritional value:
Analysis per serving, approx:
• 2090kJ/500kcal
• 36g protein
• 30g fat
• 13g carbohydrate

Wash the fish thoroughly inside and out in cold water, dry them and make four cuts in either flank as deep as the backbone. Sprinkle with lemon juice, cover and leave to marinate. • Chop the onion and garlic finely. Skin the tomatoes and chop into quarters; remove the hard knot where the stalk joins the fruit. Wash the courgettes and cut them into rings. • Heat the oven to 200°C/400°F/Gas Mark 6. Heat 3 tbsps olive oil and fry the onions and garlic until transparent. Add the white wine and bring to the boil. Put the garlic and tomatoes in the same pan, cover and cook for 5 minutes. Season the sauce with salt and pepper. • Pour the tomato sauce into a flameproof dish and lay the fish on top. Sprinkle with the remaining olive oil, arrange the olives around the fish and bake for 20 minutes. • Scatter fresh basil leaves over the fish before serving.

Poached Salmon with Caviar Sauce

An especially delicious way to enjoy salmon

Pike Dumplings in Herb Sauce

The flesh of an old pike is particularly suitable for dumplings

4 slices of fresh salmon, each weighing 250g/8oz each
1 tbsp lemon juice
1/2 tsp salt
500ml/16fl oz water
1 tsp salt
1 bay leaf
1 tsp black peppercorns
250ml/8fl oz dry white wine
200ml/6fl oz double cream
2 egg yolks
2 tbsps dry white wine
60g/2oz black caviar
2 parsley sprigs

Preparation time: 40 minutes
Nutritional value:
Analysis per serving, approx:
• 3010kJ/715kcal
• 53g protein
• 42g fat
• 6g carbohydrate

Rinse the salmon in cold water, dry it, and rub with lemon juice and salt. • Bring the water to the boil with the salt, bay leaf and peppercorns, cook for 10 minutes, then add the wine. • Place the salmon in the stock and poach for 15 minutes over a gentle heat. • Place the salmon on a heated plate, cover and set aside. • Strain the stock, measure out 125ml/4 fl oz, mix it with the double cream and heat, stirring constantly. • Beat the egg yolks and the wine. Beat the hot cream sauce into the egg yolks in a steady stream with a whisk; stir the caviar into the sauce, pour it over the salmon and decorate with a little parsley.

750g/1lb 10oz pike trimmings
2 onions
1 bunch mixed herbs
1 bay leaf
Salt and freshly ground white pepper
2 stale bread rolls
250ml/4fl oz milk
500g/1lb 2oz pike flesh
Pinch of grated nutmeg
3 eggs, separated
200g/7oz king prawns
50g/2oz butter
50g/2oz mushrooms
1 tbsp flour
125ml/4fl oz white wine
250ml/8fl oz cream
1 bunch dill

Preparation time: 1 1/2 hours
Chilling time: 2 hours
Nutritional value:
Analysis per serving, approx:
• 2635kJ/630kcal • 39g protein
• 38g fat • 27g carbohydrate

Boil up the trimmings with 1 onion, the herbs, the bay leaf and salt and pepper in a covered saucepan. Strain and set aside. • Grate the crusts off the rolls. Soften the rolls in milk. Dice the pike flesh, squeeze out the rolls and grind very finely in a food processor. Leave to chill thoroughly for 2 hours. •Season the pike meat mixture with salt, pepper and nutmeg. Fold in the egg whites and leave to chill again. • Boil up the fish stock. • Form the fish mixture into dumplings and place in the boiling stock for 10 minutes. Heat the peeled prawns briefly in the stock. • To make the sauce, sweat the remaining diced onion in the butter, add finely chopped mushrooms, dust with the flour and thicken. Add the white wine and stock, cook for several minutes, then thicken with beaten egg yolks and cream. Finally, stir in the chopped dill.

Baked Pike-Perch

This recipe can be used for any large, whole fish

1 pike-perch, dressed and weighing 1kg/2 ¼lbs
Juice of ½ lemon
1 tsp salt
Freshly ground white pepper
1 clove garlic
1 bunch chervil
4 tbsps softened butter
2 potatoes
250ml/8fl oz vegetable stock
200ml/6fl oz crème fraîche
1 bunch dill

Preparation time: 40 minutes
Cooking time: about 35 minutes
Nutritional value:
Analysis per serving, approx:
• 2320kJ/555kcal
• 51g protein
• 31g fat
• 15g carbohydrate

Thoroughly wash the fish inside and out. Rub the body cavity with lemon juice, salt and pepper. • Heat the oven to 200°C/400°F/Gas Mark 6. • Chop the garlic finely, sprinkle it with salt then crush it with a fork. Wash the chervil, shake it dry and chop finely. Mix the butter with the garlic and chervil. Wash and peel the potatoes. Bring the vegetable stock to the boil. • Stuff the fish with the potatoes and place it in a large pan; the potatoes are there to help the fish keep its shape. Spread an even coating of chervil butter over the fish. • Bake the pike-perch on the bottom shelf of the oven for about 35 minutes. After 10 minutes, pour the hot vegetable stock around the fish. After 25 minutes, spread the fish with crème fraîche. • Wash the dill, shake it dry, remove any coarse stalks and chop finely. •Arrange the fish on a heated serving dish, pour a little of the pan juices around it and sprinkle with dill. • Delicious with young leaf spinach and hot fresh garlic bread.

Pike-Perch in a Salt Crust

A classic method for cooking fine fish

To serve 8:

1 pike-perch weighing about 2kg/4¹/₂lbs

2kg/4¹/₂lbs coarse salt

8 egg whites

60-70g/2-2¹/₂oz flour

Preparation time: 10 minutes
Cooking time: 1 hour
Nutritional value:
Analysis per serving, approx:
• 1380kJ/330kcal
• 68g protein
• 3g fat
• 9g carbohydrate

Ask your fishmonger to clean the fish. • Rinse the fish briefly under cold running water. Rub the body cavity with salt, then wash out again briefly. Dry the pike-perch on kitchen paper. • Beat the egg whites lightly and mix with the flour and salt. Take a piece of extra-strong aluminium foil about the size of a baking sheet and spread some of the salt paste on it. Lay the fish on its side on the salt. Fold all flaps of skin into the body cavity and place a piece of foil over the opening to prevent salt getting in. • Heat the oven to 250°C/450°F/Gas Mark 8. • Spread the fish evenly all over with the remaining salt paste. Bake the fish for 1 hour on the middle shelf of the oven. • Take the fish out and place it on an oval dish. Using a short-bladed knife and a small hammer or meat tenderizer, free the pike-perch from its crust. Divide into fillets and place on a heated plate. • Tastes excellent with a sauce hollandaise (see recipe) a mild cream and herb sauce or crème fraîche with garlic. Accompany with crisp French bread and a green salad.

Our Tip: Pike-perch is a fine freshwater fish though it is hard to find in Britain where it has been introduced into lakes and rivers from central Europe. However, any large freshwater fish benefits from being treated in this way . The fish must be as fresh as possible. The airtight crust of salt preserves the fine aroma and keeps the flesh delicate and juicy. Our ancestors used a similar method of preserving these qualities when cooking fish, namely by baking in a clay shell. The fish was smeared with clay and placed in a pit of glowing coals. Cooking in a salt crust has recently been rediscovered as a method in modern cuisine. In France there are recipes for chicken in a salt crust; in America, steaks are prepared in this way. Serve your guests a choice of sauces. A delicious mustard and cream sauce would be suitable and is easily prepared by mixing 3 tbsps medium mustard with some finely-chopped shallots and a carton of whipping cream. Season the sauce with salt and freshly ground white pepper.

Russian Salmon Pie

A traditional Russian recipe

To serve 6:

FOR THE FILLING:

100g/4oz buckwheat	
250ml/8fl oz water	
1 tsp sea salt	
100ml/3fl oz sour cream	
2 onions	
200g/7oz mushrooms	
50g/2oz butter	
Freshly ground black pepper	
1 tbsp lemon juice	
2 tbsps finely chopped fresh parsley	
200g/7oz smoked salmon	
4 hard-boiled eggs	

FOR THE PASTRY:

250g/8oz wholemeal flour	
1/2 tsp each of caraway seed and coriander	
50g/2oz soya flour	
Sea salt	
20g/3/4oz fresh yeast or 1 envelope dried yeast	
1 tsp honey	

250ml/8 fl oz sour cream
60g/2oz butter, diced

Preparation time: 1 hour
Cooking time: 35 minutes
Nutritional value:
Analysis per serving, approx:
• 2175kJ/520kcal
• 246g protein
• 26g fat
• 46g carbohydrate

Boil the buckwheat in water with 1/2 tsp of the salt for 5 minutes over a gentle heat. Remove the pan from the heat, cover, and leave the buckwheat to swell for a further 30 minutes. • Stir the sour cream into the buckwheat. • Dice the onions. Wash the mushrooms and slice them thinly. • Melt the butter in a pan and fry the onions until transparent. Add the mushrooms, sprinkle with the rest of the salt and some pepper, add the lemon juice and 1 tbsp of finely-chopped parsley. Cover and sweat the mixture for 10 minutes over a gentle heat, stirring occasionally. • Dice the salmon. Mix the cooked mushrooms, diced salmon and the remaining parsley into the buckwheat. Shell the eggs. • To make the pastry, mix the flour with the seasonings, soya flour and salt. Make a well in the centre of the mixture, crumble in the yeast and pour the honey over the mixture. Wait 2-3 minutes until the yeast dissolves, then add the sour cream and knead to a smooth dough. Cover the dough and leave it in a warm place to rise for 40-50 minutes. • Roll out the dough on a floured surface to a thickness of 3mm/1/8 inch. Butter a loaf tin. Cut a piece out of the dough for the lid. Line the base and sides of the tin with the pastry; trim any flaps that hang over the sides. Stir the buckwheat and mushroom mixture with a fork. Cover the base of the lined tin with about half of the filling.

Place the eggs on the mixture then spoon in the remaining filling. Cut three holes about 3cm/1 inch in diameter in the lid. Cover the tin with the reserved piece of dough to make the lid and seal it firmly all the way around the edge. Dot the lid with plenty of butter. • Place the pastry on the middle shelf of a cold oven. • Turn the oven to 200°C/400°F/Gas Mark 6. Bake for 30 minutes, switch off the oven and leave for a further 5 minutes. • The pie is at its best when hot or reheated.

Terrine of Trout

Delicate in consistency and mildly aromatic in flavour, this is an excellent dish for slimmers

To serve 8:
1 shallot
1 tsp butter
500g/1lb 2oz trout fillets
½ tsp salt
Pinch each of freshly ground white pepper and freshly grated nutmeg
40g/1¼oz wholemeal bread
250ml/8fl oz cream
100g/4oz very young carrots
15-20 balm leaves
100g/4oz shrimps
2 egg whites

Preparation time: 1½ hours
Cooking time: 50 minutes
Nutritional value:
Analysis per serving, approx:
• 855kJ/205kcal
• 16g protein
• 13g fat
• 5g carbohydrate

Clean and finely chop the shallots. Heat the butter and fry the shallots until transparent, stirring constantly; then leave to cool. • Wash the trout fillets in cold water, dry them and cut into fine strips. Season with salt, pepper and nutmeg then mix with the shallots. Process the mixture in a food processor. Leave to chill thoroughly in a refrigerator for about 20 minutes. • Dice the bread, pour half of the cream over it and leave to soak in the refrigerator. • Scrape, wash and dry the carrots, then dice them finely. Wash the balm and dry on kitchen paper. De-vein the shrimp. Wash the shrimps, drain them and chop them coarsely with the balm leaves. • Whip the rest of the cream until stiff. • Beat the egg whites until smooth and add to the chilled fish mixture with the soaked bread. Place the mixing bowl inside a larger bowl packed with ice cubes. Stir the mixture until it takes on a sheen, then fold in the whipped cream spoon by spoon. • Heat the oven to 125°C/225°F/Gas Mark ¼. Butter the terrine mould or line a loaf tin with buttered aluminium foil. • Mix the carrots and balm into the fish. Transfer the mixture to the mould or tin and smooth the surface. Seal the mould well with a lid or a double layer of aluminium foil. Fill a baking tray half-full with hot, but not boiling, water at a temperature of about 80°C/180°F. Place the terrine in this water bath and cook in the oven for 50 minutes. It is important that the water temperature is maintained at a constant 80°C/180°F. This can be checked with a sugar or roasting thermometer. • Allow the terrine to cool. Cut it into slices of equal thickness just before serving. Portions may be garnished with a wine-flavoured aspic, a few shrimps or balm leaves. To make the aspic, mix and heat equal quantities of clear fish or vegetable stock and dry white wine. Stir in the appropriate amount of softened gelatine. Leave to set in a bowl or in a dish for 3-4 hours.

Char in Aspic

A feast not only for the eyes but for the palate

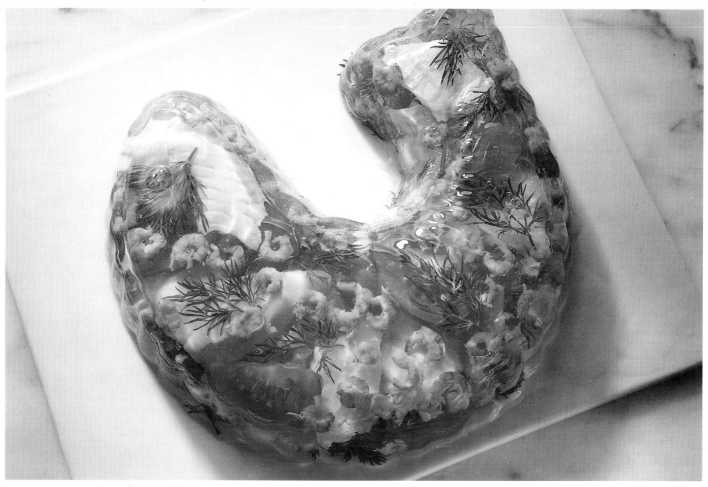

400g/14oz char fillet	
1 carrot	
2 shallots	
1 small leek	
1 stick celery	
1 bunch parsley	
1l/1¾ pints water	
Salt and freshly ground white pepper	
1 small bay leaf	
1 envelope powdered gelatine	
250ml/8fl oz dry white wine	
Pinch paprika	
200g/7oz shrimps	
1 tsp lemon juice	
1 bunch dill	
2 tomatoes	
Some lettuce leaves	

Preparation time: 1 ½ hours
Setting time: 4 hours
Nutritional value:
Analysis per serving, approx:
• 945kJ/225kcal
• 30g protein
• 2g fat
• 12g carbohydrate

Skin the char fillet, rinse the fish and dry with kitchen paper. • Scrape the carrot, peel the shallots and trim the leek and celery. Wash them thoroughly and chop them into small pieces. Wash the parsley and put it in the water with the vegetables. Cook for 20 minutes with a pinch of salt and pepper, and the bay leaf. • Poach the fish in this fumet for about 10 minutes, then remove it and set it aside to cool. Soften the gelatine in a little cold water. • Strain the fumet through a fine sieve and clarify it. In order to do this, pour in two lightly beaten egg whites into the boiling fumet and allow them to rise to the surface . Strain the fumet through muslin. Measure out 250ml/8fl oz of fumet, mix with the wine and season with the remaining salt, pepper and paprika. • Dissolve the gelatine in the hot fumet. Pour the liquid into a glass bowl and leave in the refrigerator until it begins to set. • De-vein the shrimps if necessary and wash them in cold water. Drain well and sprinkle with lemon juice. Wash and dry the dill, cut it into small sprigs and mix with the shrimps. Skin the tomatoes by plunging them in boiling water; cut them in half and remove the seeds then cut the flesh into strips of equal size. • Break up the fish and place it in the centre of the bowl. Pour some of the aspic mixture over it and leave to set in the refrigerator. Arrange the tomato strips around the fish, pour on some of the aspic mixture and leave to set in the refrigerator once more. Decorate the outer edge of the dish with dill and shrimps. Alternatively, proceed as shown in the photograph. Pour in the remaining aspic so that all ingredients are covered. • Cover the dish with aluminium foil and leave to set in the refrigerator for about 4 hours. • Wash and dry the lettuce leaves and arrange on a plate. To unmould wrap briefly in a hot damp cloth.

Our Tip: The aspic takes on a golden colour if a few saffron strands are boiled in the fumet. Instead of char and shrimps, try jellying a smoked sturgeon with freshwater crayfish. Prepare the aspic using a fumet of fish trimmings with herbs and white wine. Using moulds suitable for individual portions, build up a layer of aspic in each, allow it to set, then arrange 3 peeled crayfish and some diced sturgeon on top, garnish with dill sprigs and finally cover with more aspic.

Smoked Fish Mousses

A delicious starter

Trout Mousse
Illustrated above left

1 envelope powdered gelatine
500g/1lb 2oz smoked trout
125ml/4fl oz crème fraîche
1-2 tbsps lemon juice
Salt and freshly ground white pepper
1 head of lettuce
1 head of radicchio
3 tbsps white wine vinegar
1 tsp hot mustard
3 tbsps oil
1 shallot

Preparation time: 30 minutes
Setting time: at least 6 hours
Nutritional value:
Analysis per serving, approx:
• 1800kJ/430kcal
• 43g protein
• 25g fat
• 7g carbohydrate

Soften the gelatine for 10 minutes in cold water. • Remove the skin and bones from the trout and purée the flesh in a food processor. Add the crème fraîche, lemon juice, salt and pepper and mix together well. Dissolve the gelatine in the top half of a double boiler. Stir in some of the trout mixture. Combine this with the rest of the processed fish and season. Fill a bowl with the mousse, smooth the surface, cover and leave for at least 6 hours, or overnight, in the refrigerator. • Break up the lettuce and radicchio, wash and drain. Beat the vinegar with the mustard and oil. Peel the shallot, chop it finely and mix with the dressing. • Arrange the salad on four dishes and sprinkle it with dressing. Scoop out portions of mousse, using a spoon dipped in hot water, and arrange on the salad.

Mackerel Mousse
Illustrated above right

1 smoked mackerel
200g/7oz full-cream fromage frais
2 tbsps crème fraîche
1 small red pepper
2 shallots
1 bunch of chives
Salt and freshly ground white pepper
Pinch paprika
Juice of ½ lemon

Preparation time: 30 minutes
Chilling time: 4 hours
Nutritional value:
Analysis per serving, approx:
• 2300kJ/550kcal
• 38g protein
• 42g fat
• 4g carbohydrate

Remove the skin and bones from the mackerel, break half the fish up with a fork and purée the rest in a food processor. Whisk together the fromage frais, crème fraîche and the mackerel purée. Cut the pepper in half, remove the stalk, seeds and white pith, then wash and dry it; dice very finely, together with the peeled shallot. Wash the chives and shake them dry, then chop them finely. Set aside some of the pepper and 1 tbsp of the chopped chives as a garnish. • Stir the remaining peppers, chives and shallots into the creamed mackerel. Season well with salt, pepper, paprika and lemon juice. Stir in the mackerel flesh. Put the mousse into individual moulds and chill in the refrigerator for at least 4 hours. • Serve the mousse with a sprinkling of diced pepper and chives. • Delicious with oven-fresh white bread and a well-chilled white wine.

Fish and Vegetables in Aspic

Fish in aspic – an elegant snack for summer get-togethers

Smoked Fish with Tofu and Herb Mayonnaise

A good opportunity to get to know tofu

3 shallots	
150g/5¹/₂oz leek	
150g/5¹/₂oz carrots	
2 tbsps soya oil	
200g/7oz cucumber	
400g/14oz cod or redfish fillet	
2 tbsps lemon juice	
1 tbsp vegetable stock granules	
4 tbsps dry white wine	
2 tbsps finely chopped fresh tarragon	
100g/4oz shrimps	
125ml/4fl oz water	
3 tbsps tarragon vinegar	
2 tbsps cognac	
2 tbsps soya sauce	
1 tsp agar-agar	
1 sprig lemon balm	

Preparation time: 30 minutes
Setting time: 2 hours
Nutritional value:

Analysis per serving, approx:
• 1090kJ/260kcal
• 25g protein
• 9g fat
• 16g carbohydrate

Peel the shallots and chop them coarsely. Clean the leek and cut into rings. Wash and scrape the carrots and cut into rings, then fry them with the shallots and leeks in the oil. Wash the cucumber, cut it into strips and add to the vegetables. Chop the fish coarsely, place it on the bed of vegetables and pour lemon juice over the top. Add the stock granules, white wine and tarragon. Cover and cook for 10-15 minutes over a low heat. • Wash the shrimps and add to the mixture; transfer all ingredients to a large glass bowl. • Heat the water with the vinegar, cognac and soya sauce. Slowly whisk in the gelling agent, remove the pan from the heat, cover, and leave the liquid to stand for 10 minutes. Pour the aspic over the vegetables and sprinkle with balm leaves. • Chill before serving.

500g/1lb 2oz smoked fish	
200g/7oz tofu (bean curd)	
125ml/4fl oz water	
1 tsp soya sauce	
1 tsp mustard	
2 tsps capers	
1 tbsp lemon juice	
1 tbsp soya oil	
2 tsps apple purée	
1 small shallot	
2 tbsps finely chopped fresh herbs, such as dill, chives, tarragon and balm	
Freshly ground black pepper as required	
¹/₂ untreated lemon	
1 tomato	
Some sprigs of herbs	

Preparation time: 15 minutes
Nutritional value:

Analysis per serving, approx:
• 1485kJ/355kcal
• 30g protein
• 24g fat
• 6g carbohydrate

Arrange the fish on a serving dish and refrigerate. • Chop the tofu coarsely and purée it in a food processor, together with the water, soya sauce, mustard, capers, lemon juice, oil and apple purée. Peel the shallot and chop it finely, then add it to the sauce with the herbs. Season the tofu mayonnaise with pepper and leave it to rest for a few minutes. • Pour half the sauce over the fish and serve the rest in a sauce boat. Wash, dry and slice the lemon. Wash the tomato and cut into wedges. Garnish the serving dish with lemon, tomato and herbs. • Crackers or wholewheat bread round the dish off perfectly.

Mussels in Tomato Sauce

The mussels are cooked in the sauce itself

2kg/4¹/₂ lbs mussels
1 large onion
2 cloves garlic
1 kg/2¹/₄ lbs beefsteak tomatoes
4 tbsps olive oil
375ml/15fl oz dry white wine
¹/₂ tsp salt
Freshly ground white pepper
1 bunch basil

Preparation time: 1 hour
Nutritional value:

Analysis per serving, approx:
- 1065kJ/255kcal
- 14g protein
- 7g fat
- 17g carbohydrate

Scrub the mussels thoroughly under cold running water; remove the beards as you do so. Discard any shells that are open. • Chop the onion and garlic finely. Skin and quarter the tomatoes; remove the hard knot where the stalk joins the fruit as you do so.

Dice the tomatoes. • Heat the olive oil in a large pan and fry the onion and garlic over a medium heat, stirring constantly. Dilute with white wine and allow to boil briefly. Add the diced tomatoes, cover and cook gently for about 20 minutes. • Season the sauce with the salt and pepper and return it to the boil. Put the mussels in the sauce and cook them for about 8 minutes. Shake the pan vigorously several times during this time to ensure even cooking of the mussels. • Wash the basil and pluck the leaves from the stems. • Arrange the cooked mussels on heated plates and sprinkle with basil leaves. • Delicious with oven-fresh white bread and garlic butter.

Mussels with Mustard Mayonnaise

Serve this French dish with a dry white wine

2kg/4¹/₂lbs mussels
1 large onion
1 bay leaf
1 cup water
Freshly ground white pepper
Juice of 1 lemon
3 egg yolks
1 tbsp Dijon mustard
Salt
4 tbsps oil
2 tbsps crème fraîche
1 bunch each of fresh tarragon and chervil

Preparation time: 40 minutes
Nutritional value:

Analysis per serving, approx:
- 2300kJ/550kcal
- 62g protein
- 27g fat
- 15g carbohydrate

Scrub the mussels thoroughly under cold running water; remove the beards as you do so. Cut the onion into rings, place in a large pan with the water and bay leaf and bring to the boil. Put the mussels in the pan, sprinkle with pepper, cover, and cook for about 8 minutes; shake the pan several times during cooking. •Allow the mussels to cool in the pan with the lid removed (discard any that have not opened). Arrange the shells with the mussel flesh on a dish and sprinkle with lemon juice. • Beat the egg yolks with the mustard and salt. Add the oil, drop by drop. Mix the mayonnaise with the crème fraîche. Wash and shake the herbs dry, chop them coarsely and serve with the mussels. • Excellent with oven-crisped French bread.

Mexican Scallops

Great for a dinner party dish

32 frozen scallops with coral
Salt
Juice of $\frac{1}{2}$ lemon
$\frac{1}{2}$ bunch each of dill and parsley
1 clove garlic
2 shallots
$\frac{1}{2}$ each, green, red and yellow pepper
2 tomatoes
1 gherkin
8 tbsps oil
4 tbsps vinegar
Freshly ground white pepper
1 measure tequila (1$\frac{1}{2}$ tbsps)
Some chicory leaves
1 lime
1 dill sprig

Preparation time: 40 minutes
Marinating time: 1 hour
Nutritional value:

Analysis per serving, approx:
• 2260kJ/540kcal
• 49g protein
• 25g fat
• 24g carbohydrate

Place the unthawed scallops in boiling salted water for 8 minutes over a gentle heat, then drain them. • Place the scallop flesh in a bowl and sprinkle with lemon juice. Wash and dry the dill and parsley, then chop them finely. Peel the garlic and shallots and chop them finely too. Remove the stalks, seeds and white pith from the pepper halves, then wash and dice them. Skin the tomatoes, cut them in half and remove the seeds. Dice the tomato flesh and the gherkin. Add the herbs and prepared vegetables to the scallops and mix thoroughly. • Beat the oil with the vinegar, salt and pepper. Stir the tequila into this sauce and pour it over the scallops. Carefully toss the salad and leave to marinate for 1 hour. • Arrange the scallops with the vegetables on the washed endive leaves. Garnish with sliced lime and dill. • In Mexico, ice-cold tequila with salt and fresh limes would be served as an apéritif.

Party Dishes

A range of fondues and barbecued dishes,
not forgetting substantial fish salads
for big gatherings

Fish Fondues for Festive Fun

A fondue made with hot broth is more disgestible, but fish crisps nicely in oil

Fish Fondue in Oil

Illustrated above left

To serve 6:

300g/10oz redfish fillet	
300g/10oz salmon fillet	
300g/10oz hake fillet	
Juice of 1 lemon	
Salt	
8 king prawns	
1 lemon	
4 tomatoes	
1 bunch parsley	
1l/1¾ pints oil	

Preparation time: 30 minutes
Nutritional value:

Analysis per serving, approx:
• 1820kJ/435kcal
• 42g protein
• 30g fat
• 1g carbohydrate

Wash and dry the fillets, sprinkle with lemon juice and salt lightly. Remove any bones with tweezers. Chill the fillets in the freezer compartment of a refrigerator for a short while. De-vein the prawns. Wash them and dry them on kitchen paper. Cut the fish into cubes and arrange them on a plate with the prawns. • Cut the washed lemon into wedges. Wash and dry the tomatoes; cut them into quarters and remove the hard knot where the stalk joins the fruit. Wash the parsley and arrange it on the plate with the lemon and tomatoes. • Heat the oil in the fondue pan and place it over a spirit burner. Spike the pieces of fish on a fondue fork and dip them briefly in the hot oil. As fish can break up easily, it may be more practical to use small, long-handled conical sieves (available in Chinese supermarkets). • Delicious with bananas in curried cream, a hot paprika sauce or dill mayonnaise, and French bread or saffron rice and fresh green salad.

Fish Fondue in Chicken Stock

Illustrated above right

To serve 6:

500g/1lb 2oz sole fillets	
500g/1lb 2oz cod fillets	
Juice of 1 lemon	
Salt	
8 king prawns	
1 bunch parsley	
1 untreated lemon	
1l/2½ pints chicken stock	
125ml/4fl oz dry white wine	
Freshly ground white pepper	

Preparation time: 40 minutes
Nutritional value:

Analysis per serving, approx:
• 2300kJ/550kcal
• 38g protein
• 42g fat
• 4g carbohydrate

Wash the fish fillets in cold water, dry them, sprinkle with lemon juice and salt, then cut them into quarters. Remove the prawns' intestines. Wash the prawns in cold water and arrange them on a plate with the fish. Wash and dry the parsley. Cut the lemon into wedges. Garnish the prawns and fish with lemon wedges and parsley. • Heat the chicken stock over a spirit burner. Add the white wine. Season the stock with pepper. • Gradually cook the fish pieces and prawns in the stock. Small, coarse, long-handled Chinese sieves are perfect for the job. • Horseradish sauce or tomato, garlic and paprika mayonnaise make excellent sauces for this fondue, and French bread is a delicious accompaniment. • Serve with the same white wine used to flavour the stock.

Fish and Potato Cakes

Guaranteed to cause a stir

Fish Bread

A truly original recipe idea

To serve 8:
750g floury potatoes
5 onions
50g/2oz butter
500g/1lb 2oz mushrooms
500g/1lb 2oz tomatoes
500g/1lb 2oz cucumber
800g/1lb 12oz coley fillet
150g/5¹/₂oz soaked salted herring fillets
1 tbsp vegetable stock granules
1 tsp white pepper
500ml/16fl oz sour cream
200ml/6fl oz crème fraîche
4 eggs
4 tbsps lemon juice
1 tbsp each, of finely chopped fresh dill and parsley

Preparation time: 1 hour
Cooking time: 30 minutes
Nutritional value:

Analysis per serving, approx:
• 2135kJ/510kcal • 34g protein
• 29g fat • 30g carbohydrate

Boil the potatoes for about 30 minutes, peel them and cut into thin slices. • Dice the onions and fry in the butter until transparent. Wash the mushrooms and slice them thinly, put them in the pan with the onions, cover, and sweat for 5 minutes. Mix the mushrooms with the potato slices. • Wash the tomatoes and cucumber, peel the cucumber and dice it with the tomatoes; add to the potato and mushroom mixture. Wash the filleted coley and cut into 1cm/¹/₂-inch cubes; slice the herrings into thin strips. Mix the fish with the vegetables. Sprinkle with stock granules and pepper. Prepare a sauce using the sour cream, crème fraîche, eggs, lemon juice, herbs and the remaining pepper. • Heat the oven to 180°C/350°F/Gas Mark 4. Grease a baking sheet. • Spread the fish and potato mixture over the sheet and top with the sauce. Bake for 30 minutes until golden.

200g/7oz wheatmeal bread
500ml/16fl oz milk
2 onions
200g/7oz carrots
200g/7oz mushrooms
50g/2oz butter
Freshly ground white pepper
2 tbsps finely chopped fresh parsley
500g/1lb 2oz fillet of cod
1 tbsp lemon juice
4 eggs

Preparation time: 45 minutes
Baking time: 15 minutes
Nutritional value:
Analysis per serving, approx:
• 2340kJ/560kcal
• 41g protein
• 22g fat
• 47g carbohydrate

Cut the bread into cubes and place the cubes in a bowl. Boil the milk and pour it over the bread. Cover and leave the bread to swell, stirring occasionally. •

Dice the onions. Wash and scrape the carrots, then dice them finely. Wash the mushrooms and slice thinly. • Melt the butter in a frying pan and fry the onions until they turn transparent. Add the carrots and continue frying. Finally add the mushrooms with ¹/₂ tsp salt, the pepper and half the parsley. Cover and cook over a low heat for 5 minutes. • Wash and dry the fish, then cut it into 1cm/¹/₂-inch cubes; season with lemon juice and the rest of the salt. • Heat the oven to 200°C/400°F/Gas Mark 6. Cover a baking sheet with greaseproof paper. • Combine the cooked vegetables with the fish and eggs and the milk-soaked bread. Spread a thin layer of this mixture over the greaseproof paper and bake on the middle shelf of the oven for 15 minutes or until golden brown. • Sprinkle with the remaining parsley and slice into portions.

Herring Pie

A delicious Finnish fish pie

To serve 6:
600g/1lb 6oz fresh herring fillets
350g/11oz floury potatoes
Salt
500ml/16fl oz meat stock
100g/4oz long-grain rice
250g/8oz butter
250g/8oz flour
3 hard-boiled eggs
2 bunches of dill
White pepper
1 egg yolk

Preparation time: 1 hour
Baking time: 40 minutes
Nutritional value:

Analysis per serving, approx:
- 1715kJ/410kcal
- 15g protein
- 27g fat
- 26g carbohydrate

Soak the herring fillets for 30 minutes. • Peel the potatoes, cut them into quarters and boil for 20 to 30 minutes in salted water. • Bring the stock to the boil; put the washed rice in the stock, cover and leave over a gentle heat for 20 minutes. • Drain the potatoes, mash, and add the butter and flour and mix until smooth. Place in a refrigerator for 10 minutes. • Dry the herring fillets and cut them into strips. Separate the hard-boiled eggs into yolks and whites; mash the yolks and cut the whites into strips. Wash, dry and chop the dill. • On a floured surface, roll the potato dough into one large and one small disc. • Heat the oven to 175°C/350°F/Gas Mark 4. Butter a round tin. • Line the base and sides with the larger of the two rounds of dough. Fill the case with alternate layers of rice, herring strips, dill and egg yolk; finally sprinkle with pepper. Cover the filling with the smaller piece of dough. Brush the top of the pie with the beaten egg yolk, then, using a fork, make a number of holes in the top. Bake the pie on the middle shelf of the oven for 40 minutes. • Delicious with a fresh green salad and chopped dill mixed with melted butter.

Trout Pâté en Croûte

An elegant way of serving a delicate fish

To serve 6:

FOR THE PASTRY:

350g/11oz flour

125g/5oz clarified butter

1 egg yolk

1/2 tsp salt

4-8 tbsps ice cold water

2 eggs, separated

FOR THE FILLING:

6 fresh fillets of trout

200g/7oz plaice fillets

2 onions

15g/1/2oz butter

3 eggs

4 tbsps cream

2 tbsps breadcrumbs

1/2 tsp salt

Pinch each of freshly ground white pepper and freshly grated nutmeg

3 smoked trout fillets

1 bunch dill

Preparation time: 1³/₄ hours
Chilling time: at least 5 hours

Baking time: 1 hour 20 minutes

Nutritional value:

Analysis per serving, approx:

• 1945kJ/465kcal

• 33g protein

• 22g fat

• 32g carbohydrate

To make the dough, sift the flour into a shallow bowl, make a well in the centre and place dots of clarified butter around the edge. Place the egg yolk in the well, add the salt and water and, making sure your hands are as cool and dry as possible, knead quickly. Form the dough into a ball and refrigerate for 5 hours, or preferably overnight. • Wash and dry the trout and plaice, then cut them into fine strips. Chop the onion very finely and fry in the butter until transparent; leave the onion to cool. Mince the fish very finely in a mincer or food processor. Stir the eggs, cream and breadcrumbs

into the fish, add the onions and season with salt, pepper and nutmeg. • Heat the oven to 200°C/400°F/Gas Mark 6. Butter a loaf tin. • Roll out the dough on a floured surface and cut out 2 rectangles the same size as the tin. Line the base of the pan with one of the rectangles. Line the sides with dough and seal the seams well. Fill the pastry case with half the filling, lay the smoked trout on top and sprinkle with chopped dill. Spoon in the remaining fish mixture. Make a few holes in the dough reserved for the lid with the tines of a fork, then place the lid over the filling. Seal firmly all round the edge. Use the remaining dough for decoration. •Separate the egg yolks and whites. Brush the decorations with lightly beaten egg white and lay them on the lid. Finally brush all over with beaten egg yolk. • Bake on the bottom shelf of the oven for 1 hour and 20 minutes. • Serve either hot or cold.

Our Tip: If you are filleting the trout yourself, refer to the instructions at the beginning of the book.

Savoury Fish Flans

Piquant fish pies, unusual but especially good

Spinach and Cod Flan

Illustrated above left

To serve 6:

100g/4oz wholewheat flour
50g/2oz buckwheat flour
100g/4oz margarine
50g/2oz butter
200g/7oz low-fat quark
3 eggs • 1 tsp garlic salt
$^1/_2$ tsp black pepper
Pinch grated nutmeg
400g/14oz spinach
600g/1lb 6oz cod fillet
1 tbsp lemon juice
$^1/_2$ tsp sea salt
150g/5$^1/_2$oz coarsely grated Cheddar cheese
1 tbsp finely chopped fresh dill
25g/1oz butter, diced
1 bunch radishes

Preparation time: 30 minutes
Baking time: 40 minutes
Nutritional value:

Analysis per serving, approx:
• 2320kJ/555kcal • 37g protein
• 35g fat
• 20g carbohydrate

Mix the flours with the margarine, butter, quark, eggs and seasonings. • Wash and pick over the spinach; set aside a few attractive leaves. Blanch the spinach for 1 or 2 minutes in boiling salted water, drain it, then chop it coarsely and mix into the dough. • Wash and dry the fish, cut it into 1cm/$^1/_2$-inch cubes, season with lemon juice and salt and mix into the dough. • Heat the oven to 200°C/400°F/Gas Mark 6. Butter a 28cm/11-inch springform tin. • Press the dough into the tin and bake for 30 minutes. • Mix the cheese with the dill and scatter over the flan; dot the top with butter and bake for another 10 minutes. • Leave the flan in the tin for 10 minutes before unmoulding. Garnish with radishes and spinach and serve.

Salmon Flan with Cheese

Illustrated above right

To serve 6:

4 eggs, separated
100g/4oz wholemeal flour
100g/4oz butter
200g/7oz low-fat curd cheese
1 tsp garlic salt
2 pinches white pepper
Pinch grated nutmeg
250g/8oz spinach
150g/5$^1/_2$oz smoked salmon
400g/14oz coley fillet
2 tbsps lemon juice • $^1/_2$ tsp salt
1 tbsp finely chopped fresh dill
250g/8oz Gouda cheese
100g/4oz Cheddar or Cheshire cheese

FOR THE GARNISH:

100g/4oz smoked salmon slices
150g/5$^1/_2$oz full-fat quark
4 sprigs dill

Preparation time: 1 hour

Baking time: 35 minutes
Nutritional value:

Analysis per serving, approx:
• 2780kJ/665kcal • 51g protein
• 43g fat • 14g carbohydrate

Mix the egg yolks with the flour, butter, quark and seasonings. Blanch the spinach and chop it coarsely. Shred the salmon. Mix these into the dough. • Dice the fish fillets and sprinkle them with lemon juice, salt and dill. • Coarsely grate 150g/5$^1/_2$oz of the Gouda cheese and cut the rest into strips. Beat the egg whites until stiff. Mix the diced fish and grated cheese into the beaten egg. Heat the oven to 200°C/400°F/Gas Mark 6. • Grease a springform tin and press the dough into it. Top with the beaten egg and cheese strips. • Bake for 35 minutes. • Switch off the oven and leave the flan for a further 10 minutes. • Fill halved slices of salmon with quark and dill and arrange on top; garnish with dill.

Herrings with Apples

Excellent grilled or barbecued in foil

Grilled Pike-Perch Fillets

Unusual and refreshing in combination with lemon butter sauce

8 dressed green herrings weighing about 150g/5¹/₂oz

2 tbsps lemon juice

2 onions

4 apples

1 bunch parsley

¹/₂ tsp salt

Freshly ground white pepper

60g/2oz butter

Preparation time: 50 minutes
Nutritional value:
Analysis per serving, approx:
- 3700kJ/885kcal
- 51g protein
- 60g fat
- 24g carbohydrate

Heat the electric or gas grill or prepare the barbecue. •
Bone, wash and dry the herrings. Smear 8 pieces of aluminium foil with butter. Open out the herrings on the foil and sprinkle them with lemon juice. • Cut the onion into rings. Wash and dry the apples,

cut them into quarters, remove the cores and slice thinly. Wash, dry and finely chop the parsley. •
Season the herrings with salt and pepper, lay the onion rings and apple slices on one side of each fish. Sprinkle with parsley and dot with butter. • Fold the herrings up and grill on either side for 15 minutes. • Perfect with new potatoes and a green salad of your choice.

4 pike-perch fillets weighing about 200g/7oz, each

4 tbsps oil

4 tbsps lemon juice

4 tsps chopped fresh mint

Freshly ground white pepper

¹/₂ tsp salt

FOR THE LEMON BUTTER:

125g/5oz butter

1 tbsp freshly chopped parsley

4 tbsps lemon juice

Salt and freshly ground white pepper

FOR THE GARNISH:

4 fresh mint sprigs

Preparation time: 30 minutes
Nutritional value:
Analysis per serving, approx:
- 2110kJ/505kcal
- 38g protein
- 38g fat
- 3g carbohydrate

Wash the fillets in cold water, then dry them on kitchen paper. Combine the oil, lemon juice, mint and pepper and coat the fish with this mixture. Leave to marinate for 10 minutes. • Heat the electric or gas grill or prepare the barbecue. • Melt the butter over a low heat. Stir in the parsley, lemon juice and the salt and pepper. Heat this lemon sauce to boiling point, whisking constantly; set aside to keep warm. • Grill the pike-perch fillets on either side for 5-7 minutes, sprinkle with salt and serve garnished with the washed mint. Serve with the lemon sauce. •
Delicious with baked potatoes and a cucumber salad.

Grilled Gilt-head Bream

A delicious grilled gourmet dish

4 gilt-head bream, each weighing 400g/14oz
1 tsp salt
White pepper
2 tsps lemon juice
Pinch sugar
8 fresh balm leaves
1 onion
2 kiwi fruit
1 ripe mango
1 large cucumber
25g/1oz butter
250ml/9fl oz vegetable stock
200ml/6fl oz sour cream
Pinch garlic salt
2 tbsps olive oil

Preparation time: 30 minutes
Cooking time: 20 minutes
Nutritional value:
Analysis per serving, approx:
• 2800kJ/670kcal
• 75g protein
• 30g fat
• 25g carbohydrate

Wash the fish inside and out in cold water; dry them but do not scale them. Mix together the salt, pepper, lemon juice and sugar. Sprinkle the mixture on the inside of the fish. Wash the balm leaves and push them into the body cavity. • Peel and dice the onion, the fruit and the cucumber. • Heat the butter and fry the onion until transparent. Add the fruit and cucumber and top up with stock. Allow the liquid to reduce a little in the uncovered pan. Stir in the sour cream and season with pepper. Remove from the heat and keep the sauce hot. • Heat the electric or gas grill or prepare the barbecue. If using a barbecue, make sure that the rack is not too close to the charcoal. Brush a large piece of foil with oil and lay it on the grill rack. • Brush the fish with olive oil and grill on either side for 10 minutes. Sprinkle with oil occasionally during cooking. For the last 3 or 4 minutes, remove the foil and grill the fish directly on the rack, near the outer edge. • Before eating, strip the skin and scales from the fish. Delicious with potatoes baked in foil over charcoal.

Colourful Fish Brochettes

Halibut and plaice barbecued with vegetables and tofu

Halibut and Vegetable Brochettes with Tofu
Illustrated above left

To serve 6:
1kg/2¼lbs halibut fillets
400g/14oz tofu (soya bean curd)
3 tbsps sesame oil
2 tbsps calvados
4 tbsps dry white wine
1 tbsp soy sauce
1 tbsp apple purée
1½ limes
2 tbsps finely chopped fresh rosemary or 1tbsp dried rosemary
1 each red and green peppers
250g/8oz salad onions
Some lemon balm leaves

Preparation time: 35 minutes
Nutritional value:
Analysis per serving, approx:
• 1295kJ/310kcal • 40g protein
• 12g fat
• 8g carbohydrate

Cut the fish and tofu into 3cm/1-inch cubes. Prepare a marinade from the sesame oil, calvados, white wine, soy sauce and apple purée. Stir in ½ tsp grated lime rind. Squeeze one lime and add the juice to the marinade with the rosemary. Soak the fish and tofu in the marinade.
• Cut the peppers into eighths and remove the stalks, seeds and white pith, then wash them and cut them into 3cm/1-inch cubes. Cut the onions in half across, then cut each piece into four. Exchange the fish and tofu in the marinade for the vegetables; leave them to soak for a few minutes. • Heat the grill.
• Thread the ingredients alternately onto skewers, and include the balm leaves and a few thin slices of lime. Brush the brochettes occasionally with the marinade as you grill them for 10 minutes.

Plaice and Scampi Brochettes
Illustrated above right

To serve 6:
12 small plaice fillets
12 king prawns
3 tbsps lemon juice
6 small onions
6 tomatoes
18 mushrooms similar in size
½ bunch parsley
1 small clove garlic
25g/1oz butter
2 tbsps oil
½ tsp dried thyme
1 tsp salt
2 tsps cayenne pepper

Preparation time: 40 minutes
Nutritional value:
Analysis per serving, approx:
• 1755kJ/420kcal
• 70g protein
• 12g fat
• 8g carbohydrate

Wash and dry the plaice fillets. Shell the prawns and de-vein them. Wash the prawns in cold water then drain them. Sprinkle the fillets and the prawns with lemon juice and leave to soak. • Peel the onions and boil them in a little water for 10 minutes. • Cut the tomatoes in half and wash the mushrooms. Wash the parsley and shake it dry. Crush the garlic in a press. • Heat the grill or light the barbecue. • Melt the butter in a pan and mix it with the oil, garlic, rubbed thyme, salt and cayenne pepper. • Cut the onions in half. Place a few leaves of parsley on each of the plaice fillets and roll them up, then thread them onto skewers, alternating with the prawns, tomatoes, onions and mushrooms. • Brush the brochettes with the oil and grill on either side for 5 minutes.

Mixed Grill

Sardine and vegetables ring the changes

500g/1lb 2oz sardines
5 tbsps olive oil
2 tbsps lemon juice
2 tbsps cognac
1 tsp each finely chopped fresh or ½ tsp dried thyme and rosemary
½ tsp freshly ground black pepper
1 tsp sea salt
1 aubergine
500g/1lb 2oz courgettes
4 tomatoes
2 tbsps wholewheat flour
½ tsp ground fennel seed
20g/¾ oz butter, diced

Preparation time: 40 minutes
Nutritional value:
Analysis per serving, approx:
- 1465kJ/350kcal
- 29g protein
- 17g fat • 17g carbohydrate

Wash, clean and scale the sardines. • In a shallow dish prepare a marinade from 4 tbsps olive oil, the lemon juice, cognac, thyme, rosemary, pepper and salt. Steep the fish in the marinade. • Wash the aubergine and courgettes and cut them into slices 1cm/½ inch thick. Wash the tomatoes and cut a cross in the top of each. • Combine the flour with the fennel seeds and toss the fish in the mixture. Soak the aubergine slices in the marinade and then toss them in flour. • Heat the grill and cover the rack with foil. • Lay the sardines and aubergine slices on the foil. Toss the courgettes in the marinade and place them on the rack. Also place the tomatoes on the rack and sprinkle them with the remaining olive oil and some salt and pepper. Sprinkle the fish and vegetables with the remaining marinade and season them with salt and pepper. Dot the vegetables with butter. • Cook the sardines and vegetables under a medium grill for 5 minutes. Remove the tomatoes and set them aside to keep hot, then grill the rest of the vegetables and the fish for a further 5 minutes until tender. • Delicious with a potato or rice salad.

Salt Herrings with Oatmeal

An unusual dish, and unusally tasty

To serve 6:

750g/1lb 10oz salt herrings (including 1 soft roe)
500ml/16fl oz water
2 bay leaves
10 white peppercorns
2 allspice grains
1/2 bunch pot herbs (turnip, carrot, leek)
3 shallots
1 tbsp mustard seed
2 tsps dried dill
75g/3oz raw oatmeal
4 tbsps wine vinegar
200ml/6fl oz sour cream
100ml/3fl oz crème fraîche

Baking time: 1 day
Preparation time: 30 minutes
Marinating time: 2 days
Nutritional value:

Analysis per serving, approx:
• 1840kJ/440kcal
• 28g protein
• 31g fat
• 12g carbohydrate

Soak the herrings for 24 hours in plenty of water. • Cut the heads and fins off the herrings, then clean and fillet them. • Boil the water containing the bay leaves and seasonings for 15 minutes, strain off the liquid and return it to the pan. • Clean and wash the pot herbs and chop them finely. Peel the shallots and slice them into thin rings, then add them to the stock with the mustard seed, dill and pot herbs. Bring to the boil. • Mix the oatmeal with the vinegar and the sour cream, add it to the stock and boil for 2 or 3 minutes, stirring constantly. Remove the pan fom the stove and stir the crème fraîche and the finely chopped soft roe into the sauce. Allow the sauce to cool a little. Take a large dish with a lid and fill it in layers with the sauce and the herring fillets. • Cover tightly and leave in the refrigerator for 2 days. They will keep for about a week. • Eat with boiled potatoes in their jackets.

Swedish Pickled Herring

It's worth making twice the amount you require

500g/1lb 2oz salted Baltic herrings
4 shallots
250ml/9fl oz water
1 tsp tea leaves
125ml/4fl oz cider vinegar
2 bay leaves
10 juniper berries
5 black peppercorns
5 allspice grains
5 cloves
2 tbsps olive oil

Soaking time: 1 day
Preparation time: 30 minutes
Marinating time: 3 days
Nutritional value:

Analysis per serving, approx:
• 1505kJ/360kcal
• 25g protein
• 27g fat
• 4g carbohydrate

Soak the herrings in plenty of cold water for 24 hours. • The following day, remove the heads and fins, clean them and fillet the fish; finally slice each fillet into pieces about 4cm/1¹/₂ inches wide. Slice the shallots into thin rings. • Bring the water to the boil and pour it over the tea leaves; leave to brew for 5 minutes. Strain the tea and leave it to cool, then transfer it to a sealable container. • Add the vinegar, bay leaves, juniper berries, allspice, peppercorns and cloves. Layer the herring fillets so that they are covered by the liquid. Pour the olive oil over the top. • Delicious with potatoes boiled in their jackets or buttered wholemeal bread.

Our Tip: Leave the Baltic herrings to marinate for 3 days in the refrigerator before use. Then bottle them, in the liquid, in airtight glass jars. They should remain fresh for about 14 days. Making up a larger amount will give you a supply in case of

Pickled Herring

A welcome addition to the cold buffet

Glassblower's Herring

Illustrated above left

4 salted Baltic herrings, each weighing 250g/8oz	
125ml/4fl oz water	
125ml/4fl oz wine vinegar	
150g/5¹/₂oz sugar	
18 allspice grains	
2 bay leaves	
2 tsps mustard seed	
4 red onions	
3 carrots	
1 piece ginger	
1 piece fresh horseradish (about 5cm/2 inches in length)	

Soaking time: 1 hour
Preparation time: 25 minutes
Marinating time: 2-3 days
Nutritional value:
Analysis per serving, approx:
- 2845kJ/680kcal
- 51g protein
- 38g fat
- 31g carbohydrate

Wash the herrings and scale them with the back of a knife. Cut off the fins and tail, then remove a small strip from the belly of each fish. Make a cut between the head and the back. Separate the head from the body and at the same time carefully draw the viscera from the body cavity. Score the flank of the fish with the point of a knife and flatten the fish out on the working surface. Scrape away the dark membrane and, starting at the head end, pull the complete backbone from the fish. • Depending on the salt content, soak the herrings for about 1 hour. • Make the marinade by boiling together the water, vinegar, sugar, allspice grains, bay leaves and mustard seed; boil until the sugar is completely dissolved. Leave to cool. • Cut the onions into rings. Scrape and wash the carrots, then cut them into discs. Peel and shred the ginger and horseradish. • Dry the herrings thoroughly on kitchen paper, cut them into 2cm/³/₄-inch strips and place them in layers with the vegetables in a tall jar. Pour the cooled marinade over the top until the vegetables and fish are fully covered. • Seal the jar tightly and leave the herrings for 2-3 days in a refrigerator. • These are at their best when served as a starter with white bread or as a main course with fried potatoes.

Herrings in Burgundy

Illustrated above right

6-8 maatjes herring fillets weighing about 700g/1lb 9oz	
5 onions	
250ml/8fl oz Burgundy	
250ml/8fl oz vinegar	
200g/7oz sugar	
5 black peppercorns • 2 cloves	
4 juniper berries	
1 small piece of root ginger	
¹/₂ tsp mustard seed • 2 bay leaves	

Soaking time: 1 hour
Preparation time: 30 minutes
Marinating time: 2 days
Nutritional value:
Analysis per serving, approx:
- 2530kJ/605kcal
- 30g protein
- 40g fat
- 20g carbohydrate

Soak the maatjes fillets for at least 1 hour • Slice the onion into rings. • Make the marinade by boiling together the red wine, vinegar, sugar, and seasonings, until the sugar has completely dissolved. Add the onion rings and simmer for 5 minutes over a gentle heat. • Allow the liquid to cool then transfer it to a glass jar with the fillets. The herrings must be fully covered with the marinade. • Leave the herrings to marinate for 2 days in a refrigerator or a cold place. • This dish is excellent with potatoes boiled in their jackets or a coarse rye bread.

Marinated Mussels

Light and easily digestible - a treat for lovers of shellfish

1¹/₂kg/3lb 6oz mussels or clams	
500ml/16fl oz water	
2 tsps salt	
1 bay leaf	
1 tsp black peppercorns	
400g/14oz canned peeled tomatoes	
2 cloves garlic	
1 white onion	
3 tbsps finely chopped fresh parsley	
6 tbsps olive oil	
4 tbsps red wine vinegar	
Salt and freshly ground black pepper	
Pinch of sugar	
Pinch of cayenne pepper	

Preparation time: 1¹/₂ hours
Marinating time: 3-4 hours
Nutritional value:
Analysis per serving, approx:
• 1900kJ/455kcal
• 46g protein
• 22g fat
• 18g carbohydrate

Scrub the mussels well under cold running water, removing the beards as you do so. Discard any open shells. • Bring the water to the boil in a large pot and add the salt, bay leaf and peppercorns. Add the mussels, cover, and cook over a high heat for 5-10 minutes. Shake the pan occasionally during cooking. • Remove the mussels from the liquid and discard the bay leaf. Drain the tomatoes (retain the juice for other uses) and chop them coarsely. Chop the garlic coarsely and dice the onion. Mix the tomatoes with the onion, garlic and parsley. Stir in the oil and vinegar. Season the tomato sauce with salt, pepper, sugar and cayenne pepper. • Pour the marinade over the lukewarm mussels, mix well, cover, and refrigerate for 3-4 hours.

Maatjes-dill Morsels

Put them on cocktail sticks to serve at parties

4 maatjes herrings	
250ml/4fl oz wine vinegar	
250ml/4fl oz white wine	
200g/7oz sugar	
2 bay leaves	
1 large onion	
2 bunches dill	

Preparation time: 45 minutes
Standing time: 1 day
Nutritional value:
Analysis per serving, approx:
• 2905kJ/695kcal
• 26g protein
• 36g fat
• 56g carbohydrate

Gut the herrings through the belly and remove all traces of the dark membrane. Slit the skin on the back of the fish and pull the skin back starting at the head; remove the head and the tail. Remove the backbone starting at the tail. Soak the fillets in water for 30 minutes. • Put the vinegar, wine and sugar in a saucepan, add the bay leaves and boil until the sugar dissolves. Leave to cool. • Cut the onions into rings. Wash, dry and chop the dill. • Remove the fillets from the water, rinse them, then dry them on kitchen paper and cut them into strips. • Place the herring, onion rings and dill in a jar or deep dish, pour the cold marinade over them, cover and leave in a cool place for at least 24 hours. • Delicious with potatoes boiled in their jackets and cold beer or chilled aquavit.

Our Tip: These herring morsels will keep for several days in the refrigerator if covered or kept in a screw-top jar.

Mackerel with Juniper Berries

Something particularly delicious for special guests

Soused Herring

For fabulous summer meals outdoors

4 fresh mackerel (filleted by the fishmonger, skin left on)
12 juniper berries
1 tsp coarse salt
1 tsp each freshly ground black and white pepper
Pinch of sugar
Some lettuce leaves
1 lemon
½ bunch parsley

Preparation time: 30 minutes
Marinating time: 1 day
Nutritional value:
Analysis per serving, approx:
- 1965kJ/470kcal
- 47g protein
- 29g fat
- 5g carbohydrate

Wash and dry the fillets. Pound the juniper berries in a mortar and mix them with the salt, pepper and sugar. Cut a piece of greaseproof paper twice the width of the fillets and a little longer than them. Lay the fish on the paper, skin downwards, and sprinkle with the mixture of seasonings. Fold the greaseproof paper over and then roll it up. Arrange the fish, tightly packed together, in a dish and leave overnight. • Scrape the fish flesh away from the skin. Wash and dry the lettuce leaves and arrange them on a plate. Wash, dry and slice the lemon. Wash and dry the parsley. Arrange the fish on the bed of lettuce with the sliced lemon and parsley. • Delicious with buttered toast and a light mustard-flavoured mayonnaise.

8 small green herrings, dressed
4 tbsps lemon juice
2 onions
750ml/1 pint 3fl oz water
250ml/4fl oz vinegar
1½ tsps salt
½ tsp black peppercorns
1 bay leaf
200g/7oz sugar
6 tbsps flour
4 tbsps oil

Preparation time: 40 minutes
Marinating time: 1 day
Nutritional value:
Analysis per serving, approx:
- 3450kJ/825kcal
- 36g protein
- 47g fat
- 65g carbohydrate

Wash and dry the herrings, sprinkle them with lemon juice and leave for 10 minutes. • Cut the onions into rings. • Bring half the water to the boil with the vinegar, 1 tsp of the salt, the peppercorns, the bay leaf, sugar and onion rings; boil until the sugar is completely dissolved. Add the remaining water and leave the liquid to cool. • Mix the flour with the remaining salt and toss the herrings in it. Heat the oil in a pan and fry the herrings for 5 minutes on either side. • Put the fish in a long dish, top up with marinade, cover the dish and leave it to stand in a cool place for 24 hours. • Perfect with fried potatoes and shredded apple and carrot.

Our Tip: The fried herrings will keep in a refrigerator in an airtight container for at least 5 days in their marinade.

Marinated Fish with Vegetables

A hit with anyone with a taste for unusual dishes

Tofu and Fish with Courgettes

Illustrated above left

3 shallots • 4 tbsps olive oil	
500g/1lb 2oz courgettes	
2 tbsps vegetable stock granules	
½ red pepper	
250g/8oz tofu	
4 tbsps unsweetened apple juice	
250g/8oz cod or redfish fillet	
1 tbsp lemon juice	
1 tsp pink peppercorns	
1 tbsp finely chopped fresh or 1 tsp dried rosemary	
4 tbsps cider vinegar	

Preparation time: 30 minutes
Marinating time: 5 hours
Nutritional value:
Analysis per serving, approx:
• 1085kJ/260kcal • 19g protein
• 15g fat • 12g carbohydrate

Cut the shallots into rings and fry them in oil until they turn transparent. Dice the courgettes and fry them with the onions. Sprinkle 1 tbsp vegetable stock granules into the pan. Wash the pepper and cut it into thin strips, then add it to the pan. Cut the tofu into 1cm/½-inch cubes and put it in the pan together with the apple juice. Wash and dry the fish, add it to the pan and sprinkle it with lemon juice. Cover the pan and sweat the ingredients for 10 minutes. Season the vegetables with crushed peppercorns and rosemary. Put everything in a jar with a screw top and season with stock granules and vinegar. •
Once cool, put the jar in the refrigerator and allow the contents to marinate.

Mackerel with Vegetables

Illustrated above right

500g/1lb 2oz mackerel	
125ml/4fl oz white wine	
125ml/4fl oz water	
1 bay leaf	
1 tbsp lemon juice	
½ tsp white pepper	
2 tsps finely chopped fresh or 1 tsp dried sage	
2 onions	
200g/7oz leeks	
200g/7oz carrots	
200g/7oz courgettes	
1 red pepper	
3 tbsps sunflower oil	
250g/8oz tomatoes	
1 tbsp vegetable stock granules	
2 pinches five-spice powder	
1 tbsp finely chopped fresh or dried lovage	
3 tbsps wine vinegar	
1 tbsp Worcestershire sauce	
1 tbsp chopped parsley	
1 tsp sea salt	

Preparation time: 50 minutes
Marinating time: 1 day
Nutritional value:
Analysis per serving, approx:
• 1715kJ/410kcal • 28g protein
• 23g fat • 19g carbohydrate

Wash the fish and cut them open along their length; remove the head and backbone. Boil the trimmings with the wine, water and bay leaf for 20 minutes. • Sprinkle the fish with the lemon juice and pepper and rub the inside of the fish with sage. • Wash the vegetables and cut them into rings and julienne strips, as appropriate. • Fry the onion rings in oil until transparent, then fry the remaining vegetables for 5 minutes, stirring. Cut the tomatoes into eighths and add them to the vegetables together with the stock granules, five-spice powder and lovage. Strain the fish stock over the mixture and boil for 10 minutes. • Lay the fish on the vegetables with its skin uppermost and cook for 10 minutes, then remove it, skin it and pick out any bones. Break up the fish. • Mix the vegetables with the vinegar, Worcestershire sauce, fish and parsley. Refrigerate for 1 day.

Fish Cutlets in Piquant Marinades

Suggestions for large gatherings

Cod Cutlets in Tarragon Broth

Illustrated above left

To serve 8:

8 cod steaks, weighing 250g/8oz each

750ml/1¼ pints water

3 small bay leaves

1 tsp salt

8 peppercorns

2 tsps mustard powder

1 tbsp sugar

3 carrots

6 tbsps tarragon vinegar

300g/10oz shallots

300g/10oz small mushrooms

2 bunches dill

½ tsp white pepper

4 tbsps oil

3 fresh tarragon sprigs

Preparation time: 40 minutes
Marinating time: 1 day
Nutritional value:

Analysis per serving, approx:
- 1190kJ/285kcal • 46g protein
- 7g fat • 10g carbohydrate

Wash the cod steaks. Boil the water with the bay leaves and seasonings. Boil the scraped carrots for 10 minutes, then remove them and set them aside to cool. • Put the vinegar and the fish in the stock. Leave the steaks in the bouillon for 8-10 minutes over a low heat, then remove them and set them aside. •Slice the carrots with a crinkle cutter. Wash and slice the shallots and mushrooms. Sprinkle the mushrooms with a little tarragon vinegar. • Strain the fish stock through a sieve and add the prepared vegetables and coarsely chopped dill. Season to taste. • Place the fish in a shallow bowl. Pour the marinade and vegetables over the fish. Sprinkle with oil and garnish with tarragon. • Cover with clingfilm and refrigerate for 1 day.

Marinated Haddock Cutlets

Illustrated above right

To serve 8:

8 haddock steaks, each weighing 250g/8oz

4 tbsps flour

125ml/4fl oz oil

2 large onions

2 large carrots

3 cloves garlic

2 bay leaves

½ tsp dried thyme

125ml/4fl oz water

750ml/1¼ pints herb vinegar

3 tbsps sugar

3 tsps salt

½ tsp black peppercorns

20 stuffed olives

Preparation time: 1 hour
Marinating time: 2 days
Nutritional value:

Analysis per serving, approx:
- 1715kJ/410kcal
- 46g protein
- 17g fat
- 16g carbohydrate

Wash and dry the fish steaks, toss them in flour and fry in 4 tbsps of oil for 4 minutes on either side. • Cut the onions into rings and the carrots into strips. Chop the garlic clove finely. • Clean the pan and then fry the onion rings and garlic in the remaining oil until transparent. Stir in the carrot strips, bay leaves and rubbed thyme. Add the water, vinegar, sugar, salt and peppercorns. Boil the stock over a gentle heat for 5 minutes and then pour it over the steaks. • Cover the steaks and refrigerate for 2 days. • Cut the olives in half and scatter them over the fish before serving.

Smoked Fish Salads

These always go down well

Bloater Salad with Noodles
Illustrated above left

To serve 8:

500g/1lb 2oz wholewheat pasta	
1 tbsp salt	
500g/1lb 2oz green peppers	
500g/1lb 2oz tomatoes	
400g/14oz gherkins	
4 onions, 2 red, 2 white	
100g/4oz black olives	
500g/1lb 2oz bloaters	
2 tbsps olive oil	
2 tbsps sunflower oil	
4 tbsps red wine vinegar	
4 tbsps soya sauce	
1 tsp each sea salt and freshly ground black pepper	
3 tbsps chive rings	
3 tbsps chopped parsley	

Preparation time: 25 minutes
Marinating time: 30 minutes
Nutritional value:

Analysis per serving, approx:
- 2090kJ/500kcal
- 26g protein
- 21g fat
- 52g carbohydrate

Boil the pasta for about 10 minutes in 2l/2½ pints of salted water; drain and rinse briefly in cold water. • Cut the peppers into fine strips. Wash and slice the tomatoes. Cut the gherkins into rough cubes and the onions into rings. Chop the olives coarsely. Remove the heads, skin and bones from the fish and break them into pieces. • Put the drained pasta in a bowl with the other ingredients. • Add the oil and vinegar, herbs and seasonings and carefully mix the salad. • Leave the salad for at least 30 minutes before serving.

Mackerel and Bean Salad
Illustrated above right

To serve 8:

2 tsps vegetable stock granules	
1 tsp black pepper	
½ tsp ground caraway	
½ tsp ground coriander	
½ tsp five-spice powder	
200g/7oz bulghur wheat	
1kg/2¼lbs green beans	
2 tsps dried savory • 4 onions	
1kg/2¼lbs tomatoes	
500g/1lb 2oz smoked mackerel	
2 tbsps olive oil	
2 tbsps cider vinegar	
1 tsp garlic salt	
3 tbsps chopped chives	
3 tbsps chopped parsley	

Preparation time: 1 hour
Marinating time: 30 minutes
Nutritional value:
Analysis per serving, approx:

- 1340kJ/320kcal • 20g protein
- 11g fat • 35g carbohydrate

Bring the stock to the boil with 500ml/16fl oz water and half the herbs and seasonings. Boil the bulghur wheat for 10 minutes in this liquid. Remove the pan from the heat and leave the wheat to swell in the liquid for a further 10 minutes, allow it to cool and then break it up with a fork. • Wash the beans, cut them into 3cm/1¼-inch lengths and cook them in a little water with half of the savory for 20 minutes. • Cut the onions into thin rings. Wash the tomatoes and cut them into eighths. Put these vegetables in a bowl with the cooked beans and the wheat and sprinkle with the remaining seasonings. • Remove the heads, skin and bones from the fish, break them into pieces and add them to the vegetables, together with the oil, vinegar, garlic salt and herbs. Leave for 30 minutes before serving.

Shrimp Salads for Parties

Popular salads with gourmets, and rightly so

Shrimp Salad with Rice

Illustrated above left

To serve 10:

¹/₂ tsp salt
100g/4oz long-grain rice
400g/14oz shrimps
100g/4oz almond flakes
200g/7oz canned mandarin oranges
500g/1lb 2oz mayonnaise
125ml/4fl oz single cream
4 tbsps lemon juice
1 tsp medium mustard
3-4 tsps curry powder
¹/₄ tsp freshly grated root ginger
Pinch of sugar
2 apples
125g/5oz gherkins

Preparation time: 45 minutes
Marinating time: 1 hour
Nutritional value:

Analysis per serving, approx:

- 1800kJ/430kcal • 10g protein
- 34g fat
- 22g carbohydrate

Salt 1l/1³/₄ pints water and bring it to the boil. Wash the rice and boil it for 12-15 minutes, strain it, rinse in cold water and set aside to drain. • De-vein the shrimps then wash them in cold water and leave them to drain. • Roast the almonds in a dry frying-pan until they turn golden brown, then allow them to cool. Drain the mandarins. • Combine the mayonnaise, cream, lemon juice, mustard, curry powder, ginger and sugar. Wash the apples and cut them into quarters, remove the cores and then slice them thinly; mix the slices into the sauce. Cut the gherkins into fine strips and mix them into the apple mayonnaise together with the rice, mandarin oranges and shrimps. Cover the salad and refrigerate for 1 hour. • Stir in the flaked almonds before serving.

Shrimp and Cucumber Salad

Illustrated above right

To serve 8:

800g/1lb 12oz shrimps in their shells
1 tsp salt
4 rashers lean smoked bacon
2 tbsps oil
1 cucumber
1 bunch dill
2 tsps medium mustard
¹/₂ tsp white pepper
3 tbsps tarragon vinegar
8 tbsps sunflower oil
8 fresh lettuce leaves

Preparation time: 1¹/₄ hours
Nutritional value:

Analysis per serving, approx:

- 1045kJ/250kcal
- 18g protein
- 20g fat
- 2g carbohydrate

Cook the shrimps in boiling salted water for 5 minutes, drain and leave to cool. • Fry the bacon in its own fat until crispy, then dry it on kitchen paper. Break up the bacon into bits once it has cooled. Peel the cucumber, halve it along its length, scrape out the seeds with a teaspoon, then cut each half cucumber into slices 5mm/¹/₄ inch thick; mix it with the bacon. Wash the dill and chop it finely, then sprinkle it over the cucumber. Mix the mustard with a pinch of salt, the pepper and the vinegar. Gradually whisk in the oil as you pour it in a thin stream into the bowl. • Shell the shrimps, de-vein them and add them to the cucumber and bacon mixture. Gradually stir in the marinade. • Allow the salad to marinate for 10 minutes. • Wash the lettuce leaves, shake them dry and use them as a bed for the salad.

Rice Salad with Fish

A fresh and satisfying but low-calorie salad to complement any cold buffet

Bean Salad with Smoked Fish

Any smoked fish can be used for this dish

Rice Salad with Fish

To serve 8:
200g/7oz brown rice
500ml/16fl oz water
1 tsp salt
600g/1lb 6oz coley fillet
4 tbsps lemon juice
2 red onions
250g/8oz cucumber
250g/8oz tomatoes
250g/8oz sharp apples
3 tbsps sesame or soya oil
2 tsps garlic salt
1 tsp five-spice powder
4 tbsps finely chopped fresh dill
2 tbsps chopped chives

Preparation time: 1 hour
Marinating time: 1 hour
Nutritional value:
Analysis per serving, approx:
• 985kJ/235kcal
• 17g protein
• 7g fat
• 28g carbohydrate

Boil the rice over a gentle heat in a covered pan for 30 minutes. • Wash the fish and sprinkle it with 1 tbsp lemon juice and lay it on top of the rice. Tightly cover the pan and cook for a further 10 minutes until both rice and fish are tender. • Break the fish into pieces. Slice the onions into thin rings. Peel and dice the cucumber. Wash the tomatoes, remove the hard knot where the stalk joins the fruit and cut them into slices. Cut the apples into quarters, remove the cores and dice them. • Place all the ingredients in a large bowl, and sprinkle with the oil and remaining lemon juice. Add the garlic salt, five-spice powder and herbs and mix the salad carefully. • Leave for 1 hour to marinate before serving.

Bean Salad with Smoked Fish

To serve 10:
100g/4oz white haricot beans
100g/4oz black beans
100g/4oz aduki beans
2l/2½ pints water
1 bay leaf
2 tbsps vegetable stock granules
500g/1lb 2oz green beans
4 onions, 2 red and 2 white
500g/1lb 2oz green peppers
500g/1lb 2oz beefsteak tomatoes
500g/1lb 2oz smoked fish
4 tbsps sunflower oil
6 tbsps cider vinegar
Freshly ground black pepper
2 tsps garlic salt
2 tsps paprika
2 tsps mixed herbs
3 tbsps finely chopped fresh parsley

Soaking time: 12 hours
Preparation time: 1 hour
Marinating time: 30 minutes
Nutritional value:

Analysis per serving, approx:
• 1295kJ/310kcal
• 18g protein
• 17g fat
• 22g carbohydrate

Soak the beans in 1l/1¾ pints water overnight. • Drain them and boil in 1l/1¾ pints fresh water with the bay leaf and stock granules for 10 minutes. Wash the green beans and cut them into 4-5cm/1½-2-inch lengths and cook them with the other beans for a further 30 minutes over a gentle heat. • Drain the beans. Cut the onions into rings and the peppers into strips. Wash and dry the tomatoes, then cut them into eighths. Slice the smoked fish thickly. Make a marinade of the remaining ingredients. Mix the prepared salad ingredients together with the marinade. • Leave for at least 30 minutes before serving.

Dutch Fish and Potato Salad

Tastes delicious and goes a long way

To serve 10:

300g/10oz celery
300g/10oz chicory
800g/1lb 12oz boiled potatoes
250g/8oz Dutch cheese in 2 thick slices
800g/1lb 12oz smoked cod
125ml/4fl oz oil
1 tbsp medium mustard
5 tbsps wine vinegar
1 tsp sugar
1 tsp freshly ground white pepper
1/2 tsp salt
4 onions
2 tbsps small capers
1 bunch parsley
1 bunch chives
4 hard-boiled eggs

Preparation time: 35 minutes
Nutritional value:

Analysis per serving, approx:
- 1730kJ/410kcal
- 31g protein
- 23g fat
- 19g carbohydrate

Remove the root end and leaves from the celery and scrape off the strings. Wash the celery sticks and slice them thinly. Wash the chicory and cut it into slices. Cut the cheese into thin matchstick-sized pieces and the cod into narrow strips. Mix all these ingredients together in a large salad bowl. • Combine the oil, mustard, vinegar, sugar, pepper and salt and pour these into the salad bowl. Dice the onions finely. Chop the capers coarsely. Wash and dry the parsley and chives and chop them finely. Stir these into the salad. • Peel the eggs, cut them into eighths and use them as a garnish for the salad.

Delicious Fish Salads with Fruit

A real delicacy if you use wild rice

Astoria Fish Salad

Illustrated opposite top

To serve 10:

2 heads celery

4 tbsps lemon juice • 1 tsp salt

1kg/2¼lbs hake fillet

100g/4oz raisins

1kg/2¼lbs apples

100g/4oz shelled walnuts

800ml/1¼ pints sour cream

1 tbsp honey • 2 tbsps mustard

1-2 tsps garlic salt

3 tbsps chopped parsley

5 tbsps mayonnaise

Preparation time: 40 minutes
Nutritional value:
Analysis per serving, approx:
• 1045kJ/250kcal • 20g protein
• 11g fat • 16g carbohydrate

Cut the celery into pieces, including the hearts. Cook for 10 minutes in 1l/1¾ pints of salted water with 2 tbsps lemon juice and the fish. • Flake the fish. Wash the raisins in hot water. Dice the apples. Chop the nuts coarsely. Mix with the other ingredients.

Orange and Fish Salad

Illustrated opposite below

To serve 8:

800g/1lb 12oz cod or redfish fillets

3 tbsps lemon juice

250g/8oz wild rice (or long-grain)

1 tbsp oil • 500ml/16fl oz water

750g/1lb 10oz oranges

3 white onions

2 tsps dried oregano

2 tbsps chopped parsley

200ml/6 fl oz cream • 1 tsp salt

Preparation time: 30 minutes
Nutritional value:
Analysis per serving, approx:
• 1505kJ/360kcal • 23g protein
• 13g fat • 40g carbohydrate

Sprinkle the fish with 1 tbsp of lemon juice. • Add the oil to the water and boil the rice for 10 minutes; add the fish and cook for a further 10 minutes. • Cut the oranges into slices and the onions into rings and mix them and the other ingredients into the rice.

Fine Fish Sauces

Cream and White Wine Sauce

This sauce is appropriate for delicately textured fish. Variations can be made by adding a pinch of saffron, 1 or 2 tsps anchovy paste, 4 tbsps of freshly-chopped herbs or chopped mushrooms, or by substituting orange juice for the fish stock.

In an open pan over a medium heat, reduce 125ml/4fl oz of dry white wine and a similar amount of fish stock by about a half. Add 100ml/3fl oz crème fraîche and reduce over a gentle heat, stirring continuously.

Sauce Hollandaise

A delicate sauce suitable for fine fish and shellfish. It can be turned into a Chantilly or mousseline sauce by adding 3 tbsps whipped cream. For a maltaise sauce beat the egg yolks with orange juice (preferably from blood oranges) instead of wine and, at the last minute, sprinkle with some finely-grated orange peel.

Melt 200g/7oz butter in a pan over a gentle heat. Skim off the foam then remove the pan from the heat. In a small bowl, beat together 2 eggs yolks, 4 tbsps white wine and the juice of half a lemon

Beurre Blanc

A classic butter sauce, lighter than hollandaise but every bit as traditional in fish cuisine. Beurre blanc (white butter sauce) goes well with poached fish and fried fillets or steaks.

Chop 5 shallots very finely then boil them with 125ml/4 fl oz dry white wine over a gentle heat, stirring continuously until the liquid has nearly evaporated. There should be just enough liquid remaining to moisten the shallots.

Sauce Rémoulade

Rémoulade or tartar sauce can be bought ready-made, but compared with the home-made version it is rather ordinary. The sauce is good with fried fish, breaded fish fillets and all types of smoked fish.

Finely chop 1 small onion, 1 small gherkin, 1 anchovy fillet, $1/2$ a bunch of parsley, the leaves of 2 chervil sprigs, 2 tarragon sprigs and 2 teaspoons of capers.

Stir 25g/1oz butter into the hot sauce until the sauce and butter are fully combined. Season the sauce with salt, freshly ground white pepper and a pinch of sugar, if desired. Do not allow to come back to the boil.

Whip 125ml/4fl oz double cream into soft peaks. Remove the sauce from the heat and fold in the cream. Pour the sauce into a sauce boat and sprinkle it with about 2 tsps fresh, chopped herbs, such as basil, dill, chervil, parsley or chives.

In a large pan, boil water for a water-bath, bain-marie or double boiler. Reduce the heat and place the bowl containing the egg mixture into the water-bath; the water must gently seethe but should not come to the boil again. Stir the egg mixture until it is smooth and creamy, making sure that no water gets into the bowl.

Remove the egg yolks from the water-bath and stir in the melted butter, drop by drop at first, but gradually increasing the amount. Season with salt and freshly-ground white pepper and serve immediately.

Gradually add 100g/4oz chilled, diced butter and beat with a whisk. Reduce the heat a little as you do so. When all the butter has been used heat the sauce to just below boiling point, stirring constantly and season with salt and freshly ground white pepper.

Remove the sauce from the stove. Whip 3 tbsps of cream until it just begins to stiffen and fold it into the sauce. Pour the sauce into a sauce-boat and serve immediately.

Beat 2 egg yolks with 1 tsp mustard and, drop by drop, add 125ml/4fl oz of cold-pressed olive oil until a smooth mayonnaise is obtained. When about half the oil has been added, the rest can be poured in as a thin stream.

Season the mayonnaise with a pinch of salt and sugar if desired, then mix it with the chopped herbs and season again; add further flavourings if desired, including lemon juice.

Recognising Fish and Shellfish

The following notes are intended for anyone interested in finding out about the choice of fish, and not just for those who like good cooking and food. We have restricted ourselves to descriptions of the most important species that are available in the shops. Each species appears with its English name, and most of the names are also given in French, German, Spanish and Italian. However, fish names vary greatly from place to place, both within the English-speaking world and in Europe, so no claims are made for absolute accuracy in all cases. Indications are also given as to where the varieties are caught, in what condition they should arrive at market, suitable ways to prepare them, and in which combinations they taste best. As for the question of harmful substances contained in the seas which, because of increasing pollution, may be consumed when eating fish, an expert states: 'Harmful substances occurring in minute amounts in sea fish are found in similar amounts in other foodstuffs and give no grounds for discrimination against fish as a valuable element in the diet'.

The Herring Family

Fish of this family live in shoals. All members of the family are slim, have a single dorsal fin, small pectoral and ventral fins and thin, loose scales. Shoals live in deep oceans and in coastal waters. The best-known members of the group are the shad, herring, Baltic herring, anchovy, sardine and sprat. There are many other types which are not of great significance to the fishing industry. The shad, which swims up rivers to its spawning grounds, is the only migratory member of the group.

Shad

Fr: alose; Ger: Alse; Ital: alaccia; Span: sabalo.
At a minimum of 50cm/18 inches in length, the shad is the largest of the herrings. Shoals chiefly live in the coastal waters of western Europe, North America and the Mediterranean. A catch of shad on its way to the spawning grounds is especially prized as it will include a well-developed and delicious roe. The shad is relatively oily and has scales.

Cooking Methods: Prepare shad fillets in the same way as pike, salmon, trout and sole. Trimmings can be used for stocks or soups. Scaled and gutted shad can also be fried. It is tossed in flour, batter or egg-and-breadcrumbs for deep-frying, grilled in aluminium foil or poached in a stock with onions and sorrel.

Sauces and Side Dishes: freshly grated horseradish, anchovy butter, asparagus; Sauce Hollandaise or Sauce Rémoulade (page 108).

Herring

Fr: hareng; Ger: Hering; Ital: aringa; Span: arenque
Herrings are oily fish with scales which average 30cm/12 inches in length. They are caught from the Bay of Biscay to the Arctic Ocean. The North Sea and the Baltic varieties are smaller because these seas have a lower salt content, but the fish are more succulent. Herring are caught at three different stages of maturity: immature fish, in which the soft roe (male) or roe (female) has not formed, are known as maatjes herrings, from the Dutch word. They are caught in May and June. The periods for catching mature herrings fall between July and August and December and April. Because mature herrings are caught before spawning, the soft roe and roe are well developed. In the autumn herring, the reproductive organs have shrunk considerably, and the fish is much less oily than the maatjes and mature herring, but the flesh is especially tasty. These are caught between September and October. Herrings tend not to be sold fresh in any great numbers; most are preserved ready to eat. These range from Bismarck herrings, which are strips of fish preserved in a vinegar marinade or rollmops, which are strips rolled with gherkin, onions or sauerkraut, to Brat-herring, which are gutted herring, fried unboned and preserved in vinegar. There are also bloaters – lightly salted hot-smoked herring – fried herrings for immediate consumption or home-preserving, and kippers which are cold-smoked salted maatjes herrings. Other types available are green herring, which are young, fresh fish, Kronsardine, the industry name for the smallest herring from the Skagerak, fillets, salted herrings and pickled maatjes herrings, which are the immature fish preserved in salt.

Cooking Methods: Fresh herrings must be scaled and gutted and, where appropriate, also filleted. They are usually shallow fried after having been tossed in flour or breadcrumbs,

Sea Fish

or grilled. The fish may be stuffed with mushrooms or shallots (mixed with the soft roe if possible) or simply with herbs. They can be fried without a coating, brushed with a seasoned oil or grilled in aluminium foil. Herrings can also be oven-baked in foil with stock, vegetables and seasonings or served au gratin with breadcrumbs and butter.

To remove the extreme saltiness of salted herrings, they must be soaked in water or milk before use, depending on the recipe, for at least an hour and preferably overnight. Smoked, salted or marinated herrings are especially suitable for cocktails or salads. Herring fillets are excellent in a cold mayonnaise sauce with slices of apple and onion rings.

<u>Sauces and Side Dishes:</u> Herb butter, mustard butter, grilled tomatoes, fried onions, crispy bacon with fresh herrings; for salted and pickled herrings green beans and fried or boiled potatoes, and sour cream or yogurt. Serve herrings with generous wedges of lemon.

Anchovy

Fr: anchois; Ger: Sardelle; Ital: acciuga; Span: anchoa.
The anchovy is an oily fish found in the Atlantic, Black Sea and above all, the Mediterranean. It grows to a length of between 9cm/3½

inches and 15cm/6 inches. Because of their perishability, anchovies are only sold fresh near coasts, and are otherwise frozen, salted, smoked or preserved in oil.

<u>Cooking Methods:</u> Fresh or frozen anchovies can be scaled and fried in breadcrumbs or batter, tossed in flour and fried, boned and stuffed with chopped herbs or wrapped in vine leaves or Swiss chard and poached in white wine.

<u>Sauces and Side Dishes:</u> Grilled tomatoes, spinach; cream and wine sauce.

Sardine

Fr: sardine; Ger: Sardine; Ital: sardina; Span: sardina.
The sardine is an oily fish recognisable by its silvery colour and fairly large scales; it grows up to 25cm/10 inches in length. It lives in the Atlantic from the Canaries to the waters around Norway, and in the Mediterranean. Sardines are most widely available canned in oil, but are often available frozen and occasionally fresh.

<u>Cooking Methods:</u> Sardines can be scaled and fried in breadcrumbs or batter, baked with a little white wine, diced tomatoes and coated in breadcrumbs or stuffed with mushrooms and shallots, sprinkled with parsley and baked au gratin, or grilled in aluminium foil. Serve with lemon wedges.

Sprat

Fr: esprot, sprat; Ger: Sprotte; Ital: spratto; Span: sprat
Shoals of this oily fish are found in the Black Sea, Baltic, Mediterranean and the North Atlantic. The sprat grows to between 10cm/4 inches and 17cm/6½ inches in length. It is generally available in smoked form and is rarely available fresh or frozen.

<u>Cooking Methods:</u> Use any method suitable for sardines. Smoked sprats, or sprats in oil or a marinade can be used for starters or buffets.

The Cod Family

Fish of this family are white with very small scales and a long body. Some types carry small barbs on their lower jaw. The most important types are the blue ling, cod, ling, pollack, haddock, hake, coley and whiting. The main fishing grounds for cod are in the Atlantic between Great Britain and Iceland, Canada and Newfoundland, and also the North Sea and Baltic.

Blue Ling

Fr: lingue bleu; Ger: Blauleng; Ital: molva allumgata; Span: maruca.
Blue ling is a sub-species of the ling recognisable by the shiny metallic colouring on its back. It is restricted to northern waters. Although sometimes available fresh, it is usually subjected to an open-air drying process before going on sale.

<u>Cooking Methods:</u> The fresh, filleted fish is usually fried in batter. Dried blue ling must be thoroughly soaked before use, after which it may be used in stews or speciality dishes.

Baltic Cod

Fr: tancaud; Ger: Dorsch; Ital: merluzzo; Span: bacalao.
This type weighs on average about 1kg/2¼lbs.
<u>Cooking Methods:</u> Fillets are usually tossed in flour or breadcrumbs and fried. Cut into cubes it can be used in casseroles and fricassées. Whole fish can be baked either in the pan or wrapped in foil with a little white wine stock. Spread some crème fraîche, sour cream or thick-set yogurt on the fish before the cooking time is up.
<u>Sauces and Side Dishes:</u> Young leaf spinach with wild herbs, sweetcorn, crispy bacon and diced tomatoes.

North Atlantic Cod

Fr: cabillaud; Ger: Kabeljau; Ital: merluzzo fresco; Span: bacalao.
One of the most important species for the fishing industry worldwide. The cod has three large dorsal fins and its lower jaw is heavily barbed. Mature fish can reach a length of 1m/3 feet and weigh up to 20kg/45lbs. North Sea cod generally weigh only 6-7kg/13-15lbs. The main fishing grounds for cod are coastal areas in the North Atlantic. Cod is sold in pieces, fillets or steaks. In Scandinavia, gutted, salted and dried cod, known as Klipfisk (the air-drying process was traditionally carried

Recognising Fish and Shellfish

out on the cliffs) is commonly available. Dried salt cod, also known as stockfish, is a feature of the cooking of many regions, including Portugal, southern France and the Caribbean. Dried cod should always be soaked for at least 24 hours in several changes of water before use. Smoked cod can be used like smoked haddock.

Cooking Methods: Fresh cod should always be scaled. Its delicate and tasty flesh only requires a short cooking time; baking, frying, poaching and steaming are all suitable methods, and cod can also be made into dumplings. When baking large pieces of cod use foil. When deep-frying or shallow-frying cod, cracker crumbs or matzo meal make a better coating than actual breadcrumbs. Curry, tarragon, garlic, parsley and anchovy paste are ideal seasonings.

Sauces and Side Dishes: Cooking apple, green beans, mushrooms, cheese, leeks, carrots, peppers, beetroot, gherkins, fried bacon, spinach, tomatoes, onions.

Ling

Fr: lingue; Ger: Lengfisch; Ital: molva; Span: allunga, maruca. The ling is a long, slim fish. Its rear dorsal fin and its anal fin both stretch half the length of its body; it has a prominent barb on its lower jaw and no scales, and grows to a length of 1.5-2m/4½-6 feet. The main fishing grounds are the Atlantic from the English Channel to Norway, and the North Sea.

Cooking Methods: Ling is usually available in fillets. It can be baked in breadcrumbs, added to soups or stews or minced and made into fishcakes.

Sauces and Side Dishes: Any strongly-flavoured vegetables; well-seasoned sauces.

Pollack

Picture below
Fr: lieu jaune; Ger: pollack; Ital: merluzzo giallo; Span: abadejo. Pollack is a relative of the cod but grows to a length of no more than about 60cm/2 feet. It lives in the Atlantic around western European coasts, and also around Iceland and in the western Mediterranean. The firm flesh is coloured pink and used to make imitation crabmeat.

Cooking Methods: Any recipe that calls for cod.

Haddock

Fr: aiglefin; Ger: Schellfisch; Ital: nasello; Span: merluza.
An important fish for the European and American fishing industries. It lives in the North Atlantic and as far north as the Arctic Ocean, and in the North Sea. It grows up to 50cm/20 inches in length and weighs from 2-3kg/4½-6lbs. Fresh haddock is generally sold whole, in pieces and in steaks or as fillets. Smoked haddock is delicious mixed with rice in a kedgeree or poached and served with a poached egg.

Cooking Methods: Use any method suitable for cod; it must be scaled. Haddock is delicious poached in a wine or herb stock.

Grill or fry the steaks in butter after marinating them for a short time in milk. Basil, dill, bay leaf, horseradish, parsley, saffron, leeks and lemon are suitable seasonings.

Sauces and Side Dishes: Oysters, mushrooms, shrimps, vegetable julienne, herb butter, mussels, gherkins, anchovies, tomatoes, onions; sauce hollandaise (page 108), caper sauce, mustard sauce.

Hake

Fr: colin, merlus; Ger: Seehecht; Ital: luccio marino; Span: merluza
This slim fish has the powerful jaws of a hunter; it grows to between 50cm/20 inches and 1m/3 feet in length and can weigh up to 10kg/22lbs. It hunts over a wide area of the western Atlantic, stretching from Iceland to the coasts of Africa and South America, but also inhabits the North Sea.

Cooking Methods: Hake must be scaled. Prepare whole fish or pieces in the same way as haddock or cod. The firm, white flesh is well suited to fondues and brochettes as well as soups and fricassées. Cayenne pepper, capers, garlic, freshly chopped herbs, sage, shallots, mustard and truffles are suitable seasonings.

Sauces and Side Dishes: Chopped hard-boiled eggs, sorrel purée, breadcrumbs browned in butter, shallots poached in red wine, fried diced bacon, fried onions.

Coley

Fr: grélin; Ger: Seelachs; Ital: merlano nero, merluzzo

carbonaro; Span: gado, palero. The waters around Iceland, the coast of Greenland, Newfoundland, Norway and the east coast of America are the main fishing grounds for coley, which is getting a growing share of the world market now that the more popular white fish are becoming so expensive. The coley grows to a length of about 1m/3 feet. It is generally sold in fillets. It is smoked or pickled in oil as an economical substitute for salmon.

Cooking Methods: Any recipe that calls for cod. Coley must be scaled. Smoked or pickled coley is suitable as a starter, in mixed fish dishes, as a salad ingredient or in sandwiches.

Whiting

Fr: merlan; Ger: Wittling; Ital: merlano, nasello; Span: merlan, pescadilla.
The whiting grows to about 50cm/20 inches and chiefly inhabits the Atlantic from the Straits of Gibraltar to Lofoten off Norway, the Mediterranean and the Black Sea. Because its firm, white flesh is easily damaged by freezing, it is generally only available in a fresh condition near coasts. It is particularly delicious when smoked.

Cooking Methods: Whole fish should be scaled. Fillets may be fried in batter or tossed in flour or breadcrumbs. Whole fish can be poached in a fish and white wine stock with shallots or baked in foil in the oven. Whiting is also baked au gratin with a breadcrumb, grated cheese and butter topping. Dill, garlic, parsley and lemon are good seasonings.

Sea Fish

Sauces and Side Dishes:
Oysters, mushrooms, shrimps, strips of lettuce, fennel julienne, mussels, fried parsley, asparagus tips, grilled tomatoes, truffles, fried onions, onion purée; beurre blanc (see page 108), herb sauce, tomato sauce.

Spiny-Finned Fish (Acanthopterygii)

This is a fairly small group whose main members are the true mackerel and tuna. The mackerel family includes the frigate mackerel which is a deep-sea fish found in the Atlantic. Tuna, bonito and bonitol are all members of the family and have the same characteristic body shape. They are among the oiliest of fish.

Mackerel

Picture below
Fr: maquereau; Ger: Makrele; Ital: sgombro; Span: caballa.
Mackerel mainly inhabit the northern Atlantic and grow to a length of 50cm/20 inches. Their glittering blueish-green colouring grows paler after they are caught. The mackerel's tasty and juicy flesh makes it a popular fish. Its share of the market is comparable with that of cod. Smoked and canned mackerel have been available for many years and the fresh product is increasingly available.
Cooking Methods: Fresh mackerel require scaling and may be filleted, depending on the dish. They may be cooked whole and because of the high oil content, braising, grilling or poaching are to be preferred. They can also be poached in pieces and served with a butter sauce. A traditional English recipe calls for poaching in a fennel stock and serving with a sauce made of puréed gooseberries. The classic recipe for grilled mackerel fillets includes croûtons fried in anchovy butter. Mugwort, dill, fennel tops, garlic, cress, parsley, anchovy paste, shallots and lemon are suitable seasonings.
Sauces and Side Dishes: Mushrooms, green peas, vegetable julienne, herb butter, mussels, celery, onion purée; hot herb sauce, tomato sauce and white wine sauce.

Redfish

Fr: rascasse du nord, chèvre, sébaste; Ger: Rotbarsch; Ital: scorpena rossa, scorfeno roso; Span: gallineta nordica.
The redfish, also known as Norway haddock, is a squat, striking red fish with dark marbling on its back and a long row of spiny dorsal fins; the head is large and it has a protruding lower jaw. The redfish lives in the oceans of the northern hemisphere. It grows to about 50cm/20 inches in length and weighs 1-2kg/2¼-4½lbs. Its tasty firm flesh is not too oily. Redfish is usually available in fillets rather than as a whole fish.
Cooking Methods: Any recipe that calls for cod. Redfish must be scaled.

Tuna

Fr: thon; Ger: Thunfisch; Ital: tonno; Span: atun.
Tuna grow up to 2.5m/8 feet in length and can weigh up to 100kg/230lbs. It lives in all the world's oceans and is a very fast swimmer. Canned tuna in oil or brine has been a familiar product for many years, but tuna is increasingly available fresh in steaks or fillets.
Cooking Methods: Fresh tuna is usually sold with the skin removed. If the skin remains attached, it must be scaled. The firm flesh makes it excellent for frying au naturel, tossed in flour or breaded; grilling is also a suitable method. Fillets can also be deep fried in batter or breadcrumbs. Large pieces can be steamed over a white wine and veal stock (use the reduced steaming liquid to make a sauce). The combination of tuna and veal is best known in the classic Italian dish 'Vitello Tonato'. Curry, capers, garlic, marsala wine, parsley, basil and lemon are suitable seasonings.
Sauces and Side Dishes: green peas, carrot strips, gherkins, anchovies in oil, shallots, diced raw ham, diced fried bacon, tomatoes, onions, caper sauce, anchovy sauce, sauce rémoulade (page 108), tomato sauce.

Bonito

Fr: bonite; Ger: bonito; Ital: tonno bonita.
This relative of the tuna grows to only 1m/3 feet or so in length and may weigh 10kg/23lbs. It lives in nearly all the world's oceans, but predominantly inhabits the Mediterranean and the Atlantic. It is often sold as 'Skipjack tuna'.
Cooking Methods: Any that are suitable for tuna. Bonito must be scaled.

Bonitol

Fr: boniton; Ger: Bonitol; Ital: tonnina
A smaller cousin of the bonito that lives only in the Mediterranean. Its flesh is firmer and tastier than the flesh of the bonito.
Cooking Methods: Any that are suitable for tuna. Bonitol must be scaled.

Albacore

Fr: germon; Ger: Germon; Ital: tonno alalunga
The albacore is a type of tuna which grows to about 1m/3 feet in length; it inhabits the Mediterranean and the waters of the Caribbean. It is highly sought-after because of its firm and tasty flesh.
Cooking Methods: Any that are suitable for tuna. Albacore must be scaled.

Flat Fish

Flat fish are very similar to each other in shape and habits. Over the course of their development they have adapted to life on the sea bed. Their eyes, for example, are both set on the same side of their head, the side that is uppermost. Underneath, the fish are plain and pale-coloured, but the uppermost

Recognising Fish and Shellfish

skin is camouflaged by imitating the colours of the surroundings. Flounder, brill, halibut, lemon sole, plaice, sole and turbot are members of this group.

Flounder

Fr: flet; Ger: Flunder; Ital: passera; Span: platija.

The flounder mainly lives in shallow European coastal waters. It grows to between 30-40cm/12-16 inches in length. Some specimens have been known to live for 40 years, by which time they have become correspondingly large. Fresh flounder does not appear in the shops very often, although in smoked form it is highly sought-after.

Cooking Methods: Any method suitable for plaice. The flounder does not require skinning before use, but the darker skin can be removed if desired. It is always served with the lighter skin uppermost. A gourmet will remove the slightly thicker top skin.

Brill

Fr: barbue; Ger: Glattbutt; Ital: rombo liscio; Span: barbadar.

The brill has a smooth skin without hard protrusions and its body is more circular than oval in shape. It lives in the shallow waters of the Mediterranean and the Atlantic, and buries itself in the soft sea bed.

Cooking Methods: Brill does not require skinning before it is cooked. It can be cooked whole in a dry white wine or stuffed; other methods include poaching in a fish and wine stock, deep-

frying in batter or au gratin. Some recipes call for the skinned fillets to be fried in oil or butter. Dill, tarragon, capers, parsley, rosemary and lemon are suitable seasonings.

Sauces and Side Dishes: Oysters, leaf spinach, melted butter, mushrooms, tarragon butter, shrimps, diced fresh cucumber, leek, julienne of carrot, mussels, shallots, asparagus tips, tomatoes; beurre blanc (page 108), sauce hollandaise, cheese sauce.

Halibut

Fr: flétan; Ger: Heilbutt; Ital: halibut, fletano; Span: mero.

Halibut live in deep waters in the northern Atlantic around Greenland, Iceland and Spitzbergen, off the east coast of North America, and in the northern Pacific.

White Halibut is the largest of all flat fish, growing to an average length of 1m/3 feet; mature fish can reach 2m/6 feet or even 4m/13 feet in length. They can weigh up to 100kg/230lbs and in exceptional cases, up to 300kg/700lbs. These facts account for the halibut's importance to the fishing industry. Halibut flesh is light in colour, tasty but less delicate than brill or turbot.

Cooking Methods: Halibut can be poached or fried, skinned or unskinned, usually in pieces. Steaming and sweating are particularly suitable methods. For serving at a dinner party they are normally filleted.

Bouquet garni, tarragon, capers, bay, parsley and lemon are suitable seasonings.

Sauces and Side Dishes: Artichoke hearts, melted butter, grated cheese or breadcrumbs and butter for halibut au gratin, mixed herbs, mussels, fried bacon, grilled tomatoes; Chantilly sauce, anchovy sauce, wine sauce.

Black Halibut is a smaller cousin of the white variety; by contrast its flesh is rather oily. It mainly lives in Arctic waters and grows to about 1m/3 feet in length; it may weigh anything up to 18kg/40lb.

Black Halibut is highly prized for its delicate flavour. The fine quality of smoked black halibut has long been recognised.

Cooking Methods: Black halibut is excellent when foil-baked with a little wine and seasonings; its flavour is generally like that of white halibut.

Lemon Sole

Fr: limande sole; Ger: Rotzunge; Ital: sogliola limanda; Span: limanda, mendo limon.

The top skin of the lemon sole has a reddish tinge. It lives around the European and American Atlantic coasts.It can reach a length of 50cm/20 inches and a weight of 1kg/2 1/4lbs. Its flesh is white, tasty and not very firm.

Cooking Methods: Any method suitable for plaice. Parsley, mustard and lemon are suitable seasonings.

Sauces and Side Dishes: melted butter, chopped hard-boiled eggs, shrimps, breadcrumbs browned in butter, sauce hollandaise (page 108), white wine sauce.

Plaice

Picture below

Fr: carrelet; Ger: Scholle; Ital: passera; Span: platija.

The reddish-orange blotches on the upper skin and fins of the plaice are its hallmark. It lives all over the North Atlantic, around Europe's Atlantic coasts and in the North Sea and Baltic. It ranges in length from 20-40cm/8-16 inches and is the most common flat fish in the shops. Its flesh is light, tasty and soft.

Cooking Methods: Fry and deep-fry. Toss whole plaice or fillets in flour, bread them lightly or - for fillets in particular - dip them in batter. Capers, chervil, garlic, white pepper, thyme and lemon are suitable seasonings.

Sauces and Side Dishes: Melted butter, shrimps, lettuce strips with tomatoes and pineapple chunks, herb butter, black olives, anchovy butter, anchovy fillets in oil, diced fried bacon, grilled tomatoes, sauce hollandaise (page 108), tomato sauce.

Sole, Dover Sole

Picture below

Fr: sole; Ger: Seezunge; Ital: sogliola; Span: lenguado.

This delicious variety is the most popular of all flat fish but turns up relatively seldom in a catch, which accounts for the high market price it commands. The main fishing grounds for Dover sole are around the Atlantic coasts of Europe and as far

Sea Fish

south as North Africa, and the Mediterranean. Dover sole grow up to 50cm/20 inches in length and generally weigh between 200-500g/7-18oz.

Cooking Methods: Sole may be cooked whole after being skinned, or in fillets after being lightly scaled. They may be poached in a fish and wine stock or in a red wine with shallots. Fry sole after tossing the fish in flour, crushed crackers, or matzo meal; they can also be deep-fried in batter. Large whole fish can be baked in foil in the oven. To preserve the sole's own delicate flavour, use a light seasoning of basil, dill, fennel leaves, kirsch, parsley, port, paprika, anchovy paste, thyme or truffles. A middle cut of Dover Sole is best dotted with butter and grilled, then served with a herb sauce on the side or with grapes.

Sauces and Side Dishes: Artichoke hearts, sliced aubergine, oysters, melted butter, mushrooms, mushroom purée, shrimps, pike stuffing, herb butter, fried sliced pumpkin, fried wild mushrooms, mussels, julienne of peppers, grated Parmesan cheese, beef marrow, scampi, shallots, green asparagus tips, leaf spinach, fried diced tomato and banana, tomato purée, onion purée, grapes; Béchamel sauce, curry sauce, sauce hollandaise (page 108), tomato sauce, white wine sauce.

Turbot

Fr: turbot; Ger: Steinbutt; Ital: rombo, rombo chiodata, rombo gigante; Span: rodaballo.
Turbot is a flat fish with hard, bony growths in its upper skin. It grows to about 1m/3 feet in length and can weigh up to 40kg/90lbs; smaller examples are, however, more common. Its main habitats are Atlantic coasts from Norway to the Mediterranean. It has firm, tasty flesh.

Cooking Methods: Before cooking, the upper skin of a turbot is always removed; the fish may be completely skinned if desired. Small fish should be poached in a mixture of milk and water, or fried after being tossed in flour or breadcrumbs. They may also be prepared au gratin in the oven with a sauce. Larger fish are usually filleted or cut into portions. Curry, tarragon, capers, garlic, parsley, paprika, saffron and lemon are suitable seasonings.

Sauces and Side Dishes: Apple slices fried in butter, melted butter, tarragon butter, shrimps, herb butter, julienne of celeriac and carrot, mussels, diced peppers, anchovy butter, anchovy fillets, leaf spinach, baked, fried or grilled tomatoes, whiting stuffing, fried onion rings, onion purée; herb sauce, cream sauce, white wine sauce.

The Bream Family

Fish of the bream family that can be found in shops include gilt-head bream, red bream and pandora bream. They all have a slightly squat body and typical blunt head. They are highly-prized in Mediterranean cooking.

Gilt-head Bream

Fr: daurade, vraie daurade; Ger: Goldbrassen; Ital: orata; Span: dorada.
The gilt-head bream inhabits the Mediterranean and African Atlantic coasts. The gilt-head is not an oily variety. It grows to a length of 30-50cm/12-20 inches. Its flesh is fine in texture and its aromatic flavour makes it a prize catch.

Cooking Methods: Small examples can be tossed in flour and fried whole after scaling. For fillets use the recipes given for sole. Large gilt-heads can be foil-baked in the oven with vegetables or a little fish and wine stock, and stuffed if desired.

Red Bream

Fr: pageau; Ger: Rotbrassen; Ital: fragolino, pagello fragolino. This variety of sea bream can be recognised by the red colouring on its back.

Cooking Methods: Any recipe that calls for gilthead bream.

Pandora Bream

Fr: pagre; Ger: roetlicher Brassen
This variety also lives mainly in the Mediterranean but is often found in warmer fluvial waters, especially the Nile.

Cooking Methods: Any method suitable for carp. Pandora bream must be scaled.

Sea Fish of Other Families

Porbeagle Shark and Spur Dog

Fr: requin, squale; Ger: Heringshai, Dornhai; Ital: pescecane, squalo; Span: tiburone.
These are harmless cousins of the dangerous members of the shark family. The porbeagle can reach a length of 3m/10 feet and may weigh up to 200kg/450lbs. The main fishing grounds for the porbeagle are in the northern North Sea. Its flesh has an excellent flavour. The spur dog grows to 1m/3 feet in length and a weight of 10kg/23lbs. Smoked spur dog is very popular in Germany, where it is known as Schillerlocken. The flesh has a strong flavour. Shark is rich in protein.

Recognising Fish and Shellfish

Cooking Methods: Fillets and steaks are excellent when tossed in flour or breadcrumbs and pan-fried; they may also be deep-fried in breadcrumbs or batter. Grilling is also suitable and larger pieces can be baked in foil in the oven with vegetables and a little white wine and fish stock.

Garfish

Fr: orphie; Ger: Hornhecht, Gruenknochen; Ital: aguglia; Span: aguja.
This long, slim 'beaked' fish is caught over a wide area, from the Mediterranean to the Atlantic and also in the North Sea and Baltic. The flesh of the young garfish is very tasty but extremely bony. When smoked or fried the bones turn green. The garfish is an oily fish.
Cooking Methods: Usually skinned and served with a sauce, grilled or pan-fried.

Gurnard

Three varieties of gurnard are fished, namely the grey gurnard, red gurnard and sea swallow. Their common feature is a striking bony head and long pectoral fins. All three types grow to a length of 30-50cm/12-18 inches and live in the Atlantic from the far north to the Mediterranean; they also occur in the Adriatic. The flesh is light in colour, very tasty and not at all oily. A relatively large amount of waste results from its preparation.

Grey Gurnard

Fr: grondin gris; Ger: grauer Knurrhahn; Ital: cappone grondino; Span: triglia.

Red Gurnard

Fr: grondin rouge; Ger: roter Knurrhahn; Ital: cappone; Span: rubios.

Sea Swallow

Fr: grondin perlon; Ger: Seeschwalbe; Ital: rondine di mare.
Cooking Methods: Gurnard must be scaled. Gurnard pieces make an excellent addition to fish soups. A popular recipe for preparing gurnard whole involves stuffing the fish with shrimps and baking the fish in foil in the oven. There is also an Egyptian recipe for gurnard cut into strips and simmered in oil and white wine with leek, diced tomatoes and chopped parsley; the liquid is then mixed with garlic butter. Tarragon, capers, garlic, white pepper, leek and lemon are suitable seasonings.
Sauces and Side Dishes: Shrimps, diced cucumber, shredded lettuce, herb butter, leek and carrot julienne, shallots, grilled tomatoes and diced courgettes.

Conger Eel

Fr: congre, anguille de mer; Ger: Meeraal; Ital: grongo; Span: congrio, anguila.
The conger eel is exclusively a marine fish and does not migrate to fresh water. It is similar in appearance to the freshwater eel and like the latter, has no scales. The conger is less oily, however, and its flesh is not of comparable quality. It grows up to 2m/6 feet in length and lives to the west and south of the British Isles, in the Bay of Biscay, the Mediterranean, around the Atlantic coast of North America and around Japan and Australia.
Cooking Methods: Any method suitable for freshwater eels. It is mainly used in stews and soups. Skinned eel cut into pieces and sweated in oil, red wine and a little vinegar with chopped onions and strips of pepper is a favourite Spanish recipe. Garlic, chopped herbs, bay and thyme are suitable seasonings.

Bass

Fr: loup de mer, bar; Ger: Meerbarsch, Wolfsbarsch; Ital: spigola; Span: robélo.
This powerful, white-fleshed fish grows to a length of about 50cm/20 inches. The Mediterranean is its chief habitat, but it is also found in the Atlantic. The striped bass is closely related and lives around the North American Atlantic coast and in the Pacific.
Cooking Methods: Poach whole bass after scaling them, or else bake them in foil. The skin should be removed before serving. Cut into pieces, bass can be fried, grilled or used in bouillabaisse.

Weever

Fr: grande vive, dragon de mer; Ger: Petermaennchen, Drachenfisch; Ital: trachino dragone, vipera di mare; Span: traquino.
The weever fish takes its name from the Old French 'wivre' meaning viper; the venomous glands around its gills are responsible for this old association. They are capable of inflicting a painful sting on fishermen handling the dying fish. The weever grows to a length of 30-40cm/12-16 inches and has a small head, large mouth and spiky fins; its flesh is not oily. Its main habitat is the Atlantic coastal waters from west Africa to Bergen. The dwarf weever only reaches 10-20cm/4-8 inches in length.
Cooking Methods: Weever is mainly used in bouillabaisse and other soups and stews. Whole weever can be tossed in flour or marinated in lemon juice, oil and tarragon and then fried. Poaching in marsala is also a suitable method. Serve fried weever cold with an Italian salad. Suitable seasonings include tarragon, parsley, white pepper, sage and lemon.
Sauces and Side Dishes: melted butter, chopped hard-boiled eggs, caper sauce, julienne of fennel and carrots, herb butter, gherkins, shallots.

John Dory

Fr: St. Pierre; Ger: Petersfisch; Ital: pesce San Pietro; Span: pez de San Pedro.

Sea Fish

This fish makes good eating and can increasingly be found on sale fresh. It has an oval body with a large head and mouth and an array of spiny fins on its back. Fishing grounds are the Atlantic and Mediterranean. Its flesh is not oily and it grows to a length of 50cm/20 inches.
Cooking Methods: Any method suitable for turbot. John Dory do not require scaling.

Ray

Over 40 types of ray occur in the oceans of the world. Only the thornback ray and the skate are of any importance commercially. The wings, the wide side-pieces of the body, are the only part of the fish that is used in cooking. They are very tasty and are sold skinned, in pieces, fresh and smoked.

Thornback Ray

Fr: raie bouclée; Ger: Nagelrochen; Ital: razza chiodata; Span: raya clarata.
Its name comes from the spines along its back.
Cooking Methods: Poach fresh thornback wings in salted water, or else marinate them in lemon juice, oil, onions and herbs, then batter them and deep-fry them. They can also be foil-baked with vegetables. Suitable seasonings include basil, mugwort, Cayenne pepper, capers, bay, horseradish, parsley, pepper and lemon.
Sauces and Side Dishes: Butter heated until nut-brown (the classic French dish called 'Raie au beurre noir', strips of pepper, grilled tomatoes.

Skate

Fr: raie cendrée; Ger: Glattrochen; Ital: razza; Span: raya.
Skate live in the North Sea and the Atlantic as far north as Iceland and grow to a length of 2-2.5m/6-8 feet.
Cooking Methods: Any recipe that calls for thornback ray.

Red Mullet

Fr: rouget, rouget barbet; Ger: Rotbarbe; Ital: triglia di fango, triglia minore; Span: sargo.
Red mullet has no gall bladder and their flesh is of fine quality; it is also relatively lean. Red mullet grow to about 30cm/12 inches in length, have large scales and two barbs on the lower jaw. They mostly inhabit the Mediterranean.
Cooking Methods: Mullet are prepared whole (preferably with the scales removed) poached in a stock with a julienne of vegetables, in a fumet or in white port. Another suitable method is to toss the fish in flour and fry it. Fillets can be prepared using recipes for sole.
Sauces and Side Dishes: browned butter, mushrooms, shrimps, grated cheese, herb butter, black olives, anchovy butter, breadcrumbs browned in butter, diced fried bacon, grilled or diced tomatoes, fried onion rings; beurre blanc (page 108), curry sauce, Chantilly sauce, cream and wine sauce.

Grey Mullet

Although grey mullet and striped mullet can be found in the shops, they are not closely related to the red mullet, though they can be treated in the same way. The grey mullet reaches 30-50cm/12-16 inches in length and lives in the Mediterranean, Atlantic and North Sea. The striped mullet can grow up to 40cm/16 inches in length and lives off the coast of Madeira and around the Atlantic coasts of Africa and France.

Swordfish

Fr: espadon, empereur; Ger: Schwertfisch; Ital: pesce spada; Span: pez espada.
The swordfish grows to an average length of 4m/13 feet and can weigh up to 200kg/450lbs. It lives in nearly all the oceans of the world. The flesh of a young swordfish has an excellent culinary reputation.
Cooking Methods: Swordfish is normally sold in the form of steaks or fillets (the former will require scaling). Either may be poached in red wine or fish stock or tossed in flour and fried. All the methods listed for sole fillets are suitable for swordfish fillets. For steaks, refer to recipes for haddock.

Monkfish

Fr: baudroie; lotte Ger: Seeteufel, Anglerfisch; Ital: rospo di mare; Span: rape.
The monkfish, also known as angler fish or burbot, with its pectoral fins like arms and its powerful head with a wide mouth full of teeth, has a monstrous appearance. Although the monkfish has no scales it does have hard patches on its upper skin. The monkfish has suddenly shot to popularity thanks to its extensive use by top chefs who incorporate monkfish into many nouvelle cuisine dishes. The price has increased accordingly. Monkfish grows to about 1m/3 feet in length and lives on seabeds in all European waters. Its delicious, oil-free flesh is sometimes available smoked.
Cooking Methods: Angler fish often goes into bouillabaisse and other soups. Fillets or steaks can also be tossed in flour or breadcrumbs and fried. Refer to the notes on cod for suitable seasonings and sauces.

Catfish, Wolf Fish

Fr: loup de mer, poisson loup; Ger: gestreifter Seewolf; Ital: pesce lupo.
Catfish come in spotted and striped varieties, recognizable by the patterning on their backs. The striped variety is generally sold ready-skinned and filleted. Its flesh is light in colour, non-fatty and tasty. It is not to be confused with the American fish called a catfish, which is a freshwater variety.
Cooking Methods: Any method suitable for cod.

Freshwater and Migratory Fish

Burbot; Eel-Pout

Fr: lotte de rivière; Ger: Aalquappe; Ital: lotta; Span: lota.

Recognising Fish and Shellfish

Burbot grow to a length of 30-60cm/12-24 inches. They prefer the cool, clear waters of Europe, Asia and America. Burbot flesh is light, firm, oily, tasty and particularly free of bones.
Cooking Methods: Because the scaleless burbot has a mucous layer it can be prepared 'au bleu'. For cooking by any other method the skin should first be removed. Prepare fillets or steaks in the same way as turbot or eels.

Grayling

Fr: ombre-écailles, ombre-commun; Ger: Aesche; Ital: temolo; Span: umbra.
The grayling has an elongated oval body shape with a dark striped dorsal fin; it grows to a length of 30-40cm/12-16 inches and has lean flesh similar to that of trout. Grayling live in rivers and streams in central and eastern Europe, and also in parts of North America.
Cooking Methods: Use any method suitable for trout. Grayling must be scaled, depending on the method chosen. There are some specialist recipes for grayling. For Geneva-style Grayling the fish is poached in red wine with pot herbs and served with the reduced and thickened liquid and fried mushrooms. Lausanne-style Grayling calls for the fish to be poached in white wine with chopped mushrooms and shallots and served with the stock, enriched with butter and seasoned with lemon juice. There is also a Provençal dish of filleted grayling tossed in flour, fried in olive oil and garnished with chopped fried garlic and grilled tomatoes.

Barbel

Fr: barbeau, barbillon; Ger: Barbe; Ital: barbio; Span: barbo.
The barbel, a member of the carp family, is a long slim fish with four barbs on its lower lip. Its back is generally greyish-green and its gills a faint gold. Some barbel have an all-over reddish sheen and are called Golden Barbel. They grow to a length of 30-40cm/12-16 inches and live in fast-running rivers with clear water. During the spawning season, between May and June, they swarm upriver. During this time its roe is inedible and causes nausea. The flesh has a delicate flavour and is fat-free, however it is very bony.
Cooking Methods: Poach barbel 'au bleu' in a fish and wine stock, like trout. It can also be tossed in flour and fried, or deep fried after being breaded or battered. Fillets can be baked au gratin with a cream sauce, Parmesan cheese and butter. Tarragon, capers, chervil, garlic, bouquet garni, Dijon mustard and lemon are suitable seasonings.
Sauces and Side Dishes: Herb butter, black olives, grilled tomatoes; horseradish, mussel or cream and wine sauce.

Perch

Fr: perche; Ger: Barsch; Ital: pesce persico; Span: perca.
Perch is fat and oval in appearance with stiff spiny fins and dark stripes across its body. Perch can reach a length of 60cm/24 inches and a weight of 2kg/4 ½lbs. Perch live in streams, rivers, lakes and brackish waters all over northern Europe, northern Asia and North America. The flesh is delicate with a low oil content and has a pleasant taste.
Cooking Methods: Perch must be scaled. Small fish can be prepared in the same way as trout or fried in batter. Larger fish should be braised with herbs and a little white wine.
Sauces and Side Dishes: Mushrooms, chopped hard-boiled egg with parsley and browned butter, green peas, shrimps, anchovy butter, asparagus tips; sauce hollandaise (page 108).

Bream

Fr: brème; Ger: Blei, Brasse; Ital: sarago, abramide comune; Span: sargo.
The bream is a densely-scaled, handsome fish related to the carp, and shares the body shape typical of other members of that family. It grows to about 50cm/20 inches in length, may weigh up to 3kg/7lbs and lives in all the European inland waters north of the Alps. Although it is bony, the flesh is delicately flavoured, albeit with a high fat content.
Cooking Methods: Use any method suitable for carp. Bream must be scaled. Suitable seasonings include mugwort, dill, caraway, horseradish, black pepper, sage, stonecrop and lemon.
Sauces and Side Dishes: Mushrooms, fresh green peas, gherkins, julienne of celeriac, leek, carrots, shallots, sour cream, onions; cream sauce.

Powan

Fr: féra; Ger: Felchen; Ital: coregone, lavaretto; Span: salmonete.
Powan have a bluish or greenish tinge and grow to a length of 30-50cm/12-20 inches; the flesh is relatively fat-free. They inhabit the large, well-aerated lakes of the Alps and northern Europe. The most famous of all are the powan from Lake Constance.
Cooking Methods: Use any method given for trout. Depending on the recipe, powan should be scaled before cooking.

Freshwater Eel

Fr: anguille; Ger: Flussaal; Ital: anguilla; Span: anguila.
Baby eels, known as elvers, measuring about 3cm/1 inch in length, swim from the deep ocean to the coast then find their way up river. They live the next 5-6 years of their lives in fresh water, growing to a length of 1m/3 feet. After that time, the mature eels return to the sea to spawn. Eel flesh has a high oil content and smoked eel is one of the finest smoked fish. Freshwater eels weighing about 1kg/2¼lbs have the tastiest flesh. Jellied eel is a favourite with Londoners and elvers are a delicacy from the River Severn.
Cooking Methods: To cook eel 'au bleu', leave the skin on. For other dishes, skin the eel by cutting a notch in the flesh all around the head end of the fish. Loop some string around the

Freshwater and Migratory Fish

notch and hang the fish on a door frame. Loosen the skin with a knife, grip it in a cloth and pull it towards the tail. Ideally, try to buy eels ready-skinned. Eels can be fried, braised in beer or cider, poached in herb stock and then served cold in their jelly, or grilled or deep-fried in flour or batter. Cayenne pepper, cognac, tarragon, capers, chervil, garlic, bay, horseradish, nutmeg, parsley, white pepper, port, sage, sorrel, mustard, sherry and lemon are suitable seasonings.
Sauces and Side Dishes: Oysters, prunes softened in white wine, mushrooms, herb butter, diced peppers, anchovy butter, shallots, asparagus tips, diced fried bacon, diced tomatoes, onions; herb sauce, cream and wine sauce (see page 108), tomato sauce.

Trout

All trout are members of the salmon family and are sub-divided according to their habitat.

Brown Trout

Fr: truite de ruisseau, truite de rivière; Ger: Bachforelle; Ital: trota di fiume, trota di torriente; Span: trucha.
Brown trout is one of the tastiest freshwater fish. It takes its colourings from its surroundings; its preferred habitats are small, fast-running rivers. It is a

non-oily species and measures 25-40cm/10-16 inches in length. Smoked trout is a delicacy.

Salmon Trout

Fr: truite saumonée; Ger: Lachsforelle; Ital: trota salmonata; Span: trucha salmonada.
The salmon trout is a migratory fish, living mostly in the northern Atlantic, Arctic Ocean, North Sea and Baltic; it returns to freshwater rivers to spawn. Its flesh is oily and highly flavoured. Adult fish range in length from 80cm-1m/32-38 inches and weigh 1-5kg/2¼-11¼lbs.

Rainbow Trout

Fr: truite arc-en-ciel; Ger: Regenbogenforelle; Ital: trota arcobaleno; Span: trucha arcoiris.
The rainbow trout is similar in appearance to the river trout, and prefers a similar habitat. Its flanks are striped in rainbow hues. It measures 25-50cm/10-20 inches in length and its flesh is non-oily. The smoked rainbow trout is a delicacy.

Brook Trout

Fr: truite lacustre; Ger: Seeforelle; Ital: trota di lago; Span: trucha lago.
The brook trout is similar to the brown variety but its flesh is less fat. It grows to an average length of 80cm/32 inches.

Cooking Methods: Trout can be prepared 'au bleu', lightly tossed in flour or breaded and served with almonds. If the fish is not to be served 'au bleu', trout should be scaled. Other good techniques include oven baking or charcoal grilling, baking with wine and vegetables, or in a foil parcel with a little wine and fish stock. Brown trout and lake trout are tasty when prepared like salmon. Suitable seasonings include dill, capers, fresh mixed herbs, parsley, white pepper, rosemary, vermouth (used in moderation) and lemon.
Sauces and Side Dishes: Oysters, melted butter, mushrooms, green beans, herb butter, carrot strips, mussels, peppers, shallots, asparagus tips, diced tomatoes, fried onions, onion purée; horseradish sauce, sauce hollandaise (page 108), anchovy sauce, cream and wine sauce.

Gudgeon

Fr: goujon; Ger: Gruendling; Ital: chiozzo; Span: gobio.
The gudgeon is a small, slim fish that grows to no more than 10-15cm/4-6 inches in length. It lives in streams, rivers and lakes throughout Europe with the exception of Scotland and southern Italy. Its light flesh is delicate and flavoursome, with a low fat content; it is, however, very bony.
Cooking Methods: After being scaled and cleaned, gudgeon can be breaded in a light crumb and fried for about 4 minutes on each side in butter. It may also be deep fried in batter or flour.

Pike

Fr: brochet; Ger: Hecht; Ital: luccion; Span: lucio.
Pike are long and round bodied with a 'duck-bill'. They inhabit the lakes of Europe and North America and lurk near the banks of slow-running streams and rivers. Adult fish are 40cm-1m/16-38 inches in length and weigh an average of 2-3kg/4½-5¾lbs. A pike weighing 10kg/23lbs is an exceptional catch. Medium-sized or younger examples are preferred for culinary use; large or old fish are suitable for stuffings or dumplings.
Cooking Methods: The word 'shaving' is more appropriate than scaling in the case of pike. Because the scales are so firmly attached to the skin, the blade of a sharp knife must be drawn along the fish from tail to head. The roe is not used. The liver imparts a pleasant tang to stuffings. Larded pike - with or without a stuffing - can be baked, or else the fish can be baked in foil with seasonings and a little white wine. If poaching, use a well-seasoned fish stock, beer with lemon, cloves, bay, peppercorns and onions, or red wine. Pike steaks may be tossed in flour and fried, braised, grilled in foil or deep fried in batter. Cayenne pepper, dill, capers, chervil, garlic, bay, horseradish, parsley, peppercorns, saffron, sage, sorrel, thyme and lemon are all suitable seasonings. Pike is often minced and made into dumplings, as in the classic French Pike Dumplings (see recipe).

Recognising Fish and Shellfish

Sauces and Side Dishes: Sliced apple, oysters, browned butter, mushrooms, chopped hazelnuts, diced celeriac, herb butter, carrot strips, mussels, peppers, anchovy butter, sorrel purée, sour cream, shallots, diced tomatoes, fried pearl onions, fried onion rings; beurre blanc (page 108), sauce hollandaise, caper sauce, white wine sauce.

Huck

Fr: huch; Ger: Huchen; Ital: huco, salmone del danubio; Span: salmon del danubio.
This long, slim member of the salmon family grows to 1.5m/4 ^{1}/$_2$ feet in length and may weigh up to 20kg/45lbs. Huck can not be found in British waters; it mainly lives in the Danube and its tributaries that rise in the Alps. Its flesh is light, oily and very tasty.
Cooking Methods: Any technique recommended for salmon. Huck must be scaled.

Carp

Fr: carpe; Ger: Karpfen; Ital: carpa; Span: carpa.
Carp live in the wild in slow-flowing or still, muddy water in rivers, streams and ponds. When purchasing fresh carp, make sure that the fish has been kept in fresh running water for 24 hours before being killed. This is to remove the taste of weed and mud. Carp occur in eastern and central Asia, the Black Sea and all over Europe, except the far north. Mirror carp and leather carp are bred in clear water. Carp grow up to 1m/3 feet in length and càn weigh up to 20kg/45lbs. The best flavour is obtained from 2-year-old fish weighing 1-2kg/2^1/$_4$-4 ^{1}/$_2$lbs. In the winter months, carp put on fat which improves their flavour. The soft roe, fried and eaten as a starter or incorporated into sauces, is a delicacy.
Carp are fried, baked or ground and made into patties or dumplings.

Common Carp

Fr: carpe commune; Ger: Schuppenkarpfen; Ital: carpa commune; Span: carpa comien. The original variety of carp, fully covered in scales.

Mirror Carp

Fr: carpe a miroir; Ger: Spiegelkarpfen; Ital: carpaspecchio.
Has a few large scales.

Leather Carp

Fr: carpe coriacée; Ger: Lederkarpfen; Ital: carpa cuoio. This variety is almost entirely without scales.
Cooking Methods: Carp are usually prepared 'au bleu' (in which case the fish should not be scaled), baked in the pan or in foil. Steaks and fillets may be baked, braised, pan-fried or deep fried in batter. The Polish style recipe with beer and red wine is a famous method (recipe on page 74).

Sauces and Side Dishes: Artichoke hearts, browned butter, mushrooms, pike stuffing, chopped almonds, horseradish, carrot, gherkins, raisins, anchovy fillets in oil, sauerkraut, sour cream, shallots, tomatoes, onions.

Salmon

Fr: saumon; Ger: Lachs; Ital: salmone; Span: salmon.
The salmon is a migratory fish that begins its life in cold clear streams and rivers. At the age of 3 years it makes its way to the sea. After about 4 years the mature salmon return to the rivers to spawn. Although it is found all over the world, it prefers colder regions. European salmon grow to about 60cm/24 inches in length and in exceptional cases to 1.5m/4 ^{1}/$_2$ feet. A good average weight is 6-8kg/13-18lbs although some examples will reach 25kg/55lbs. Its flesh varies in colour from a delicate pink to an orangey-red, it has a delicate texture and excellent flavour. Salmon is one of the most highly prized fish of all and smoked salmon is a special delicacy.
Cooking Methods: Salmon must be scaled. The Scandinavians pickle raw salmon with salt and dill (Gravadlaks). Pieces of salmon can also be braised or poached in a fish and wine bouillon. Fillets or steaks may be fried, grilled, deep fried in batter or baked in champagne. Whole poached salmon can be coated in aspic for special occasions and served cold with a fine salad and herb mayonnaise. Suitable seasonings include curry, dill, tarragon, chervil, garlic, paprika, parsley, white pepper and lemon.
Sauces and Side Dishes: Poached oysters, leaf spinach, melted butter, mushrooms, fish dumplings, deep fried milter, shrimps, diced cucumber, caviar, herb butter, cress butter, horseradish sauce, deep fried mussels, sliced olives, julienne of skinned peppers, grilled tomatoes; curry sauce, sauce hollandaise (page 108), Madeira sauce, cream-and-wine sauce.

Pollan

Fr: lavaret; Ger: Renke; Ital: lavareto; Span: coregono.
Another fish of the salmon family, but of regional interest only; it mainly occurs in the Alpine lakes of Bavaria, Austria and Switzerland but also in very deep lakes in France.
Cooking Methods: Use any method recommended for trout.

Char

Fr: omble chevalier; Ger: Saibling; Ital: salmerino alpino; Span: ombla chevalier.
The char is similar to the trout and reaches a length of 25-

Freshwater and Migratory Fish

40cm/10-16 inches, and in some cases 80cm/32 inches. It may weigh up to 10kg/23lbs. Its preferred habitat is cold, oxygen-rich fresh water, such as the lakes of the northern Alps, northern Europe, Alaska and the northeastern USA. It has a delicate, slightly oily flesh which is very flavoursome.

<u>Cooking Methods:</u> Use any method suitable for trout. Char must be scaled if they are not being prepared 'au bleu'. It can be poached in a mixture of Rhine wine, fish stock and butter with a fish and truffle stuffing (whiting or pike are suitable). The liquid is then reduced, thickened with cream and egg yolk and seasoned with crab butter.

Tench

Fr: tanche; Ger: Schleie; Ital: tinca; Span: tenca.

The tench is similar to carp and has small, deep-rooted scales covered with a mucous layer. It lives chiefly in central Europe in slow-running and heavily weeded water. Its flesh is moderately oily. It grows to a length of 20-30cm/8-12 inches and in some cases up to 20 inches; it may weigh up to 2kg/4 1/2lbs.

<u>Cooking Methods:</u> Use any method recommended for carp. Do not scale the fish if it is to be prepared 'au bleu'. Fillets and skinned slices can be used in recipes as a substitute for trout.

Sterlet

Fr: sterlet; Ger: Sterlet; Ital: sterleto; Span: sterleto.

This long slim fish has a pointed head, bony bumps on its skin and a regular row of scales on its back. It is the smallest variety of sturgeon and reaches up to 60cm/24 inches in length and a weight of 10kg/23lbs. It is rarely available in Europe because it is mainly confined to the Caspian Sea, the Black Sea and rivers flowing into it, and the rivers of northern Russia and Siberia. On the Danube it may be found as high up as Linz in Austria; it is also farmed on the Volga and in Hungary. Its flesh is delicate and finely flavoured.

<u>Cooking Methods:</u> Use any recipe recommended for pike.

Smelt

Fr: eperlan; Ger: Stint, Spierling; Ital: eperlano; Span: esperinque.

The smelt is a slim, silvery-blue fish with moderately fat flesh. It is one of the smaller members of the salmon family, reaching only 26-30cm/10-12 inches in length and a weight of 100g/4oz. It lives in coastal regions of the North Sea and Baltic, in estuaries and coastal lakes. Inland, the smelt occurs in the lakes of northern Europe.

<u>Cooking Methods:</u> Use any method suitable for sole fillets or salmon. Smelt must be scaled before cooking.

Sturgeon

Fr: esturgeon; Ger: Stoer; Ital: storione; Span: esturion.

This migratory fish lives in the estuaries of large European rivers, around the Pacific coast and in the Caspian Sea and Black Sea. Its roe is most sought-after as caviar. For this reason, sturgeon are usually caught on their upstream journey to spawning grounds. It may reach a length of 3m/10 feet and although its flesh is fatty, it is flavoursome and delicate.

<u>Cooking Methods:</u> Sturgeon is available in pieces, steaks and fillets and has no scales. Large pieces should have the cartilaginous matter removed from the back. Steaks and pieces can be poached in a white wine and fish stock, braised over vegetables or baked in foil in the oven. Steaks and fillets may be tossed in flour and fried or grilled, or deep fried in batter. One Russian recipe calls for the sturgeon to be poached in a concentrated wine vinegar bouillon, enriched with herbs and seasonings, then left to marinate in the liquid for 2 days, after which it is served cold. Suitable seasonings include tarragon, fennel, ginger, capers, garlic, marjoram, orange peel, parsley, peppercorns and lemon.

<u>Sauces and Side Dishes:</u> Buckwheat pancakes, mushrooms, fennel, grated Parmesan cheese, anchovy fillets in oil, tomatoes, onions; sauce maltaise.

Catfish

Fr: silure, glane; Ger: Wels; Ital: siluro; Span: siluro.

Central Europe's largest freshwater fish can reach a length of 1-3m/3-10 feet and a weight of 200kg/450lbs over a lifetime that may span 80 years. This scaleless fish lives in large rivers and lakes in central and eastern Europe, and there are isolated occurrences in western Asia. Young catfish in particular have a light, boneless, tasty flesh which is slightly fatty; the flesh of older fish is often tough.

<u>Cooking Methods:</u> Large pieces and steaks may be poached in a stock of wine and fish juices. Steaks and fillets can be tossed in flour or breadcrumbs and fried; deep frying in batter is also an option.

Pike-Perch

Fr: sandre; Ger: Zander; Ital: luccioperca; Span: lucigerca.

This fish is related to the perch, with which it shares the typical fan-like array of dorsal fins; it lives in European rivers and lakes, as well as some regions of the Baltic where salinity is low. It is often farmed in ponds and the commercial product from Lake Balaton in Hungary is highly esteemed. It grows to a length of 1-1.3m/3-4 feet and weighs about 15kg/34lbs. Its flesh is low in fat, delicate and very flavoursome.

<u>Cooking Methods:</u> Pike-perch must be scaled before use. Poach whole fish or pieces in a fish stock, braise them over vegetables, or bake them with a little white wine and some delicately flavoured vegetables. Steaks and fillets may be poached in a white wine and fish stock, braised, or tossed in flour or breadcrumbs and fried; deep frying in batter is also suitable. Poached fillets can be prepared au gratin with a cream sauce. Pike-perch fillets are also an excellent ingredient for dumplings or mousse. Garlic, bay, horseradish, paprika, parsley, peppercorns, sage and

Recognising Fish and Shellfish

lemon are suitable seasonings.

<u>Sauces and Side Dishes:</u>
Artichoke hearts, poached oysters, browned butter, mushrooms, chopped hard-boiled eggs, fennel, fish dumplings, celeriac, carrots, mussels, grated Parmesan cheese, anchovy fillets in oil, mustard butter, asparagus tips, glazed turnips with bacon, grilled tomatoes, onions; cream sauce.

Crustaceans

For culinary purposes, prawns, lobster, crab, crayfish and spiny lobster (langouste) are the most important members of this group. Because of commercial descriptions which frequently differ from the zoological descriptions, misunderstandings can occur. For this reason both the species name and names commonly found in the fishmonger's are given below.

Shrimps

Am: shrimp Fr: crevettes; Ger: Garnelen; Ital: gamberetti; Span: gambas.

Shrimps are marine creatures which, depending on habitat, can reach a length of 15cm/6 inches. They are sold freshly-boiled, either with or without shells, and also frozen or canned.

<u>Cooking Methods:</u> Boiled fresh shrimps must be shelled before use. The dark intestine from the shrimp's back should be removed. This is called de-

veining. Rinse them in cold water. They can be used in salads, cocktails or buffet dishes, or they may be heated briefly for use in hot dishes. Frozen shrimps should be removed from their packaging and thawed slowly in a covered container in a refrigerator.

Prawns, King Prawns

Am.: Shrimp, Jumbo shrimp Fr: crevettes roses; Ger: Riesengarnelen; Ital: gamberoni; Span: gambas.
True prawns reach a length of 17-23cm/6-9 inches.

<u>Cooking Methods:</u> Use any method suitable for scampi or Dublin Bay prawns.

Mantis Shrimp

Fr: squille; Ger: Heuschreckenkrebs; Ital: canocchie, cicala di mare; Span: galera.

This is a Mediterranean variety usually only available fresh near coasts. It is similar to the Dublin Bay prawn and grows to about 25cm/10 inches in length. Mantis shrimp tails are occasionally available frozen as 'scampi'.

<u>Cooking Methods:</u> Mantis shrimps are killed in the same way as lobsters but only require 8 minutes cooking. The proportion of flesh is relatively high thanks to its very thin shell. The aromatic flesh is delicious.

Lobster

Fr: homard; Ger: Hummer; Ital: aragosta; Span: bogavante.
Lobsters live on rocky sea beds near coasts. The tastiest are 35-45cm/14-18 inches in length and weigh 500-800g/1lb 2oz-1lb10oz. Lobsters are available live, frozen, freshly-boiled or canned as lobster meat. When buying freshly-caught crustaceans be sure that they are moving freely in their seawater tanks and that they struggle vigorously when held out of water. Any that appear damaged or dying must not be eaten as they may already be dangerous or poisonous. The tails of fresh lobsters, crayfish and spiny lobsters should be firmly curled under them.

<u>Cooking Methods:</u> If live crustaceans are not killed immediately after purchase they should not be kept on ice; this constitutes cruelty. The best method is to kill them immediately and allow them to cool in the water. They must be dead before being divided up. Lobsters and spiny lobsters (langoustes) must be plunged head first into plenty of rapidly-boiling water and held beneath the surface for at least 5 minutes. Latest research shows that under these conditions, death occurs in about 5 minutes. Have nothing to do with any recipe that

recommends killing crustaceans in simmering water. It is a known fact that this prolongs the agony of death very considerably. To kill two or more lobsters you will require a pan of at least 15l/3gallons capacity. Failing this, lobsters and spiny lobsters should be killed individually. The task is best left to an expert. A lobster weighing 500g/1lb 2oz requires 10-15 minutes cooking. Always remove frozen lobster from the packaging and thaw it in a covered dish in a refrigerator; thawing too rapidly can make the flesh tough. Boiled lobster should be cut in half lengthways, hot or after cooling. The flesh can then easily be removed from the tail, and the soft tomalley, the grey-green liver, cut from the head end. Discard the stomach-sac in the head end between the eyes. Any roe that may be found beneath the tail is a special delicacy. For a cold buffet cut the tail flesh into slices and arrange it on the lobster carcasse. Claws should be broken off and cracked open with a steak-hammer or special lobster-claw breaker. The flesh can then be removed at table.

Scampi

Eng.: Dublin Bay Prawn, Crawfish Fr: langoustine; Ger: Kaisergranate; Ital: scampi;

Crustaceans

Span: langostino.
This variety grows to 20-25cm/8-10 inches in length. Fresh, boiled tails are available in the shell, frozen flesh is usually already shelled; the flesh is also available in cans.
Cooking Methods: Shell fresh boiled tails and use them either cold or after a short period of cooking. Tails can also be grilled with the shells on or pan-fried in plenty of oil. Use the shelled tails in the same way as prawns.

Crab

Fr: crabe; Ger: Krabbe; Ital: granchio; Span: cangrechio.
Crabs are always sold freshly-boiled, never live. They have ten legs and grow to a diameter of 15-20cm/6-8 inches. They may weigh up to 6kg/13lbs. They live along gently shelving coasts from the Bay of Biscay to Norway, in the Mediterranean, on the Atlantic and Pacific coasts of North America and Alaska and in the Bahamas. Crabmeat is also available canned.
Cooking Methods: Crabmeat can be used in the same way as crayfish, lobster and spiny lobster flesh.

Crayfish

Am: crawfish, crawdad Fr: écrevisse; Ger: Krebse; Ital: gambero; Span: cangrejo.
Crayfish grow to a length of 8-15cm/3-6 inches and weigh about 100g/4oz. They are a special delicacy in Sweden and Finland and in Louisiana. Crayfish live in the mud of lakes and slow-moving rivers and streams, but they need totally unpolluted waters and for this reason they have become rare. When buying the fresh article look for the same signs as when buying lobster. Frozen ready boiled crayfish are available either peeled or in their shells; peeled crayfish flesh is available in cans.
Cooking Methods: To kill crayfish, follow the same instructions as for lobster. Use the flesh in the same way as shrimps or prawns.

Spiny Lobster

Fr: langouste; Ger: Languste; Ital: aragosta; Span: langostino.
The spiny lobster is related to the lobster but lacks the huge claws of the latter; instead it has a pair of long feelers. It prefers warmer waters to the lobster. It grows to a length of 20-50cm/8-20 inches and weighs about 1kg/2¼lbs. All the above notes on lobster also apply to the spiny lobster.

Molluscs

The molluscs include all the shellfish that are not crustaceans, whether or not they have a rigid shell, and thus embraces oysters, mussels and snails, sea urchins - which develop defensive spines - and cuttlefish - which have no protective carapace at all. Bivalves are the largest group of edible molluscs. When buying bivalves - oysters, mussels and clams - it is important to be sure that their shells are firmly shut. Because their shells contain sea water, a bivalve with a firmly shut shell can survive some days out of the sea. Molluscs which have lost their shells in the course of the ages - squid, cuttlefish and octopus - are usually only available near coasts, or frozen ready for use.

Squid

Fr: calmar; Ger: Kalmar; Ital: calamare; Span: calmara.
The squid is a cephalopod with ten tentacles. Shoals of squid are common in the Mediterranean and eastern Atlantic. They grow to a length of 30-40cm/12-16 inches.
Cooking Methods: Prepare squid in the same way as cuttlefish. The bag-like body can be stuffed with a mixture of squid tentacles, hard-boiled eggs and herbs, then fried. Connoisseurs concentrate on the tentacles which are delicate in texture. They can be sliced and fried in butter with diced onions or braised with white wine and anchovy fillets.

Octopus

Fr: pieuvre, poulpe; Ger: Meerpolyp, Oktopus; Ital: folpi, polipo; Span: poipo, pulpito.
Octopus inhabit the Atlantic and the Mediterranean. They have a round bag-like body with a large head and long tentacles. Only those up to about 1kg/2¼lbs in weight are suitable for cooking.
Cooking Methods: Prepare octopus in the same way as cuttlefish, then cook like squid.

Cuttlefish

Fr: seiche, sèche; Ger: Tintenfisch, Sepia; Ital: seppia, seppiola; Span: sepia, choco.
Cuttlefish have a flat oval body, a relatively small head and ten tentacles, two of them longer than the others. They grow to about 1kg/2¼lbs in weight.
Cooking Methods: The basic method of preparation for cuttlefish, octopus and squid is the same. Grip the body firmly and pull the head away, complete with tentacles and viscera. Take care when preparing cuttlefish not to damage the ink sac; just a small amount of ink can make the rest of the flesh inedible. On the other hand, the ink can be added to a sauce in which the cuttlefish is cooked. The porous cuttlebone or quill must also be removed from the back of the body. The tentacles are then cut

Recognising Fish and Shellfish

off just above the eyes. Remove the beak from the base of the tentacles and discard it along with the lower body and viscera. Wash the body sac and tentacles thoroughly under cold running water. The fine membrane may also be removed from the body and tentacles; this is especially recommended in the case of larger specimens. Continue preparation according to the recipe. Use cuttlefish in the same way as squid.

Oysters

Fr: huître; Ger: Auster; Ital: ostrica; Span: ostion.
Most oysters are now cultivated in artificial oyster beds. They only flourish in pure, highly saline seawater. There are various varieties of oyster, including European and Portuguese oysters. European oysters live and are cultivated on Atlantic coasts of Europe and America, and in the Mediterranean. Their shells are slightly rounded, regularly-shaped and slightly ribbed. European oysters are named after their port of origin. Thus Belgium has its Ostends, Denmark its Limfjords, Great Britain its Colchesters and Whitstables. France produces Arcachons, Belons, Bouzigues and Marennes. Holland supplies Imperials and the USA, Bluepoints. Portuguese oysters

are more irregularly shaped and have a craggy appearance. They are described according to the way in which they are cultivated, either as 'huîtres de parc' or 'fines de claires', which are a result of cultivation in a series of pools. Portuguese oysters are especially valued for their slightly tangy flavour. When oysters arrive fresh at the fish market they are classified into weight categories. Recently, Pacific oysters have come onto the market. They are twice the size of the European oyster and are sold ready-cooked.

Cooking Methods: Connoisseurs enjoy their oysters raw. The closed oysters are thoroughly scrubbed under cold running water and dried. Oysters are then opened, or shucked, with an oyster-knife, a special knife with a short, strong blade, or a strong kitchen knife. To protect the hand, the oyster should be placed with its curved surface downwards on a damp kitchen towel. The oyster knife is then applied to the 'sharp' side of the oyster and forced firmly between the two halves of the shell. Take care not to spill any of the seawater trapped inside the shell as this contributes to the oyster's delicious flavour. Run the blade of the knife under the oyster to sever the muscle and place the halves on a plate. If you do not have a special oyster plate with indentations, pour a layer of salt about 1cm/½ inch deep over a normal

plate to prevent the oysters falling over. The oysters are then swallowed straight from the shell. The muscle that 'hinges' the two halves of the shell should be severed before serving. Some connoisseurs place a drop of lemon juice on the oyster before swallowing it, not so much as a seasoning, but as a way of testing that the oyster is still alive. If it is, the acid will cause the oyster to twitch slightly.

A meal of fresh oysters should be accompanied by fresh white bread, freshly ground pepper and a dry white wine, such as a Chablis. Oysters are also served cooked; they may be poached in their own juices and arranged in their shells for serving. In this case serve a cream sauce with the oysters. Or smear the shells with oil and put the poached oysters back in them, sprinkle with a fine crumb, some Parmesan cheese, chopped parsley and dots of butter, then bake them. They can also be wrapped in thinly-sliced bacon and grilled on skewers. Fried oysters are served inside thick wedges of French bread in New Orleans; this delicious snack is called La Médiatrice.

Cockles

Fr: coque; Ger: Herzmuschel; Ital: cuore edule; Span: berberecho, croque.
Cockles have dark and light stripes on their shells. They occur in the Mediterranean and

on the Atlantic coasts of France and Great Britain, usually in shallow waters around estuaries. Common cockles reach 4-5cm/1¾-2 inches in diameter.

Clams

Fr: palourde, coque bucarde; Ger: grosse Herzmuschel; Ital: cuore tubereolato; Span: concha.
This type grows to 5-8cm/2-3 inches in diameter. Clams are especially popular in the United States, where they form the basis of the classic fish soup from the north-eastern states, Clam Chowder. The clam flesh is cooked with potato and onion in a cream-and-herb stock. In some places, tomato purée is added.

Molluscs

Spiny Cockles

Fr: coque épineuse; Ger: dornige Herzmuschel; Ital: cuore spinosa; Span: concha.
The ribs on the shell of this type have small spines; it grows to 4-5cm/1¾-2 inches in diameter.
Cooking Methods: Near coasts cockles are eaten raw like

Crustaceans

oysters; they may be prepared and cooked in the same way as mussels.

Scallops

Fr: coquille St Jacques; Ger: Jakobsmuschel; Ital: conchiglia San Giacomo, pellegrina; Span: vieira.

Scallops inhabit the Atlantic, Mediterranean and the North Sea. They measure 8-15cm/3-6 inches across. The shell is an attractive beige or pinkish colour with regular radial ribs. Near coasts, scallops are available fresh but elsewhere they are available frozen.

Cooking Methods: Allow frozen scallops to thaw gradually in a refrigerator. Wash the shells and break them open like oysters. Remove them from the shell and separate the whitish-yellow muscle and the pink coral from the other organs, which are greyish. Blanch the muscle and coral in a sieve in lightly boiling water for 2 or 3 minutes, slice them and continue with the recipe as directed. After blanching, the scallop flesh can be deep fried in breadcrumbs or batter, served in a sauce, au gratin, or grilled on skewers with bacon. Cayenne pepper, curry powder, dill, mango chutney, white pepper, dry sherry and lemon are suitable seasonings.

Sauces and Side Dishes: Mushrooms, shrimps, grated cheese, mussels, diced tomatoes; cream and wine sauce.

Mussels

Fr: moule commune; Ger: Miesmuschel; Ital: mitilo, musculo; Span: concha, mejilon. The mussel is blackish-blue, oval and tapering in shape and grows to a length of 5-6cm/2-2½ inches. It secures itself to rocks and piers by means of a byssus, a beard-like mass of strong threads that grow from within the shell. Mussels prefer a habitat of steeply shelving water up to a depth of 10m/32 feet. It occurs in all European and North American waters. By far the majority of mussels on the market are farmed. The brown mussel is a relative of the common type.

Cooking Methods: There are a number of recipes for mussels in this book. Fish soups and stews are often supplemented by mussels. Suitable seasonings include Cayenne pepper, tarragon, fennel leaves, chervil, garlic, bay, paprika, parsley, sherry, thyme, Worcestershire sauce and lemon.

Sauces and Side Dishes: Mushrooms au gratin, peppers, rice, shallots, streaky bacon, celery, tomatoes, onions; cream sauce.

Carpet Shell

Fr: clovisse, palourde; Ger: Teppichmuschel; Ital: vongola nera; Span: almeja margarita. Carpet shells are found in the Atlantic, the Mediterranean and the English Channel. They grow to 3-5cm/1¼-2 inches across and have ribbed shells with three radial rows of spots.

Cooking Methods: Use any method suitable for mussels. On the coast, carpet shells may be eaten raw, like oysters.

Venus Shell

The following are two types that live in the Atlantic and the Mediterranean.

Smooth Venus

Fr: palourde, praire; Ger: braune Venusmuschel; Ital: vongola dura; Span: almeja. This has an elongated shell with brown radial bands; it grows to 5-7cm/2-3 inches across, and in exceptional cases up to 12cm/5 inches across.

Warty Venus

Fr: coque rayée, praire; Ger: rauhe Venusmuschel; Ital: cappa verrucosa, tartufo di mare; Span: escupina gravada. This variety only grows to about 3-5cm/1¼-2 inches across; its shell is characterized by its irregular bumps.

Cooking Methods: Any method suitable for mussels. At coastal locations they may be eaten raw, like oysters.

Venus shells are usually sold simply under the name of 'clam'.

Index

A

albacore 113
anchovy 111
    Jansson's Temptation 60
apple(s):
    herrings with 93
    rolled fish with 49
Arabian-style Perch 66
asparagus, & fish in aspic 38
aspic:
    char in 81
    fish & asparagus in 38
    fish & vegetables in 83
Astoria Fish Salad 107
'au bleu':
    cooking fish 9, 10-11
    eating fish 14
    trout 51
au gratin:
    fish 65
    lobster 41
    scallops 39
    scampi, with cucumber 31
avocados, stuffed 34

B

bacon:
    catfish in 72
    trout in 72
bakes:
    cauliflower & fish 56
    redfish & tomato 56
baking 12
Baltic cod 111
barbel 118
Barley Soup with Fish 23
bass 116
    in red sauce 33
batter 13
bean sprouts, redfish fillet
    with 30
bean(s):
    maatjes fillets with 48
    mackerel salad with 103
    salad with smoked fish 105
Beurre Blanc 108
Bismarck herring 110
black halibut 114
bloater 110
    salad with noodles 103
    toasts 28
blue ling 111
bonito 113
bonitol 113
Bouillabaisse 63

C

braising 10
Brat-herring 110
bread, fish 89
bream:
    freshwater 118
    sea 115
        Tuscan style 75
    see also gilt-head bream
brill 114
brochettes:
    halibut & vegetable, with
        tofu 95
    plaice & scampi 95
brook trout 119
brown trout 119
burbot 117-18

C

cabbage, Savoy:

fish roulade 61
Canapés with Mackerel Cream 26
caper sauce, halibut steaks in 48
carbohydrates 7
carp 120
    Oriental style 74
    Polish-style 74
carpet shell 125
catfish:
    freshwater 121
    in bacon 72
    sea 117
    stuffed 64
Cauliflower & Fish Bake 56
caviar sauce, poached salmon
    with 76
char 120-1
    in aspic 81
charcoal grill 12-13
cheese, salmon flan with 92
Chinese Deep-fried Scampi 73
Chinese Fish & Rice 65
Chinese Fish
   Soup 20
clam 124
    chowder 62
cleaning fish 8
clear soups 21
cockles 124
cocktails:
    lobster 35
    prawn 35
    shrimp 35
    spring 34
cod 111-12

Cauliflower & Fish Bake 56
cutlets in tarragon broth 102
dried 112
fillets, devilled, with
    broccoli & tomatoes 44
Fish Fricassée 47
Fish on Cress 28
fish soup, Chinese 20
    cream 23
flan, with spinach 92
in wine sauce 55
smoked 112
    & potato salad, Dutch 106
Solyanka 20
with tomatoes 67
coley 112
    fish dumplings 21
    rice salad with 105
    with spinach 34
    with tomatoes 67
conger eel 116
consommé, French 25
cooking methods 10-13
courgettes, tofu & fish with 101
court-bouillon, fish 10
crab 123
crackers, fish 28
crayfish 123
    in aspic 81
    soup, classic 18
        cream, cold 18
cream sauce:
    mussel ragoût in 52
    with white wine 108
cress, fish on 28
crustaceans 7, 122-3
cucumber:
    & dill soup with shrimp 19
    scampi au gratin with 31
    shrimp salad with 104
Curried Prawns 47
cuttlefish 123-4
    deep-fried 46

D

deep frying 12
Devilled Cod Fillets 44
dill:
    -maatjes morsels 99
    sauce, shrimps in 52
    soup with fish dumplings 21
Dover sole 114-15
dumplings:
    fish 21
    pike 76
    smoked salmon 21
Dutch Fish & Potato Salad 106

E

eating fish & seafood 14
eel, freshwater 118-19
    see also conger eel
eel-pout 117-18

F

fat 7
filleting fish 8-9
fish:
    & rice, Chinese 65
    & tofu with courgettes 101
    au gratin 65
    bake, with cauliflower 56
    barley soup with 23
    consommé, French 25
    crackers 28
    dumplings 21

    fillet, Florentine 44
        'Tre Verde' 70
    fricassée 47
    in aspic, with asparagus 38
        with vegetables 83
    mould, Norwegian 58
    on cress 28
    pan-fried 53
    rice salad with 105
    rolls, in herb sauce 45
        in tomato sauce 49
        with sliced apple 49
    roulade 61
    salad, with orange 107
    soufflé with millet 30
    stew, with mussels 58
    sweet & sour 33
fish cakes, with potato 89
flan:
    salmon, with cheese 92
    spinach & cod 92
flat fish 113-15
    filleting 9
    skinning 8
flounder 114
foil 12
fondue:
    in chicken stock 88
    in oil 88
French Fish Consommé 25
freshwater fish 117-22
frozen fish 7
frying 12

G

garfish 116
garlic butter, king prawns in 39
gilt-head bream 115
    grilled 94
    Roman style 75
Glassblower's Herring 98
Gravad Lax 36
grayling 118
green herring 110
    stuffed 53
grey gurnard 116
grey mullet 117
grilling 12
gudgeon 119
gurnard 116

H

haddock 112
    cutlets, marinated 102
    Norway *see* redfish
    Pan-fried Fish 53
    smoked 112
    with melted butter 55
    with tomatoes 67
hake 112
    Astoria Fish Salad 107
halibut 114
    brochettes with vegetables
      & tofu 95
    foil-baked 71
    steaks in caper sauce 48
herb:
    sauce, fish rolls in 45
      pike dumplings in 76
herring(s) 110
    Fish Crackers 28
    Glassblower's 98
    green 110
      stuffed 53
    in Burgundy 98
    maatjes 110

    cocktail 27
    -dill morsels 99
    fillets with green
      beans 48
    with mustard 26
    pickled, Swedish 97
    pie 90
    salt, with oatmeal 97
    soused 100
    with apples 93

with spicy mayonnaise 32
Hollandaise Sauce 108
hors d'oeuvre 27, 30-1
horseradish sauce, smoked
    trout with 36
huck 120

J

Jansson's Temptation 60
John Dory 116-17
juniper berries, mackerel
    with 100

K

king prawns 122
kippers 110

L

leather carp 120
lemon sole 114
    skinning 9
ling 112
    blue 111
lobster 122
    au gratin 41
    cocktail 35
    Dijonnaise 41
    see also spiny lobster

M

mackerel 113
    cream, canapés with 26
    mousse 82
    pan-fried, with tomatoes 54
    salad, with beans 103
    with juniper berries 100
    with vegetables 101
main courses 43-67
mantis shrimp 122
Matelote 60
mayonnaise:
    mustard 84
    spicy 32
    tofu & herb 83
melon, spiny lobster tails with
    37
Mexican Scallops 85
millet, fish soufflé with 30

mirror carp 120
Mixed Grill 96
molluscs 123-5
monkfish 117
mould, Norwegian 58
mousse:
    mackerel 82
    salmon, special 38
    smoked fish 82
    trout 82
mullet 117
mussel(s) 125
    chowder 62
    eating 14
    in tomato sauce 84
    marinated 99
    ragoût in cream sauce 52
    risotto 61
    soup, cream 24
    stew, with fish 58
    with mustard mayonnaise 84
mustard:
    Lobster Dijonnaise 41
    maatjes herrings with 26
    mayonnaise, mussels with 84

N

noodles, bloater salad
    with 103
North Atlantic cod 111-12
Norwegian Fish Mould 58
nutritional value 7

O

oatmeal, salt herrings with 97
octopus 123
omelettes, shrimp 29
Orange & Fish Salad 107
oysters 124
    deep-fried 40
    Kilpatrick 40
    Rockefeller 40

P

Pandora bream 115
pâté, trout, en croute 91
Pea Soup with Shrimps 24
peppers:
    green, plaice rolls in 29
    Halibut & Vegetable
      Brochettes with
      Tofu 95

perch 118
    Arabian-style 66
pie:
    herring 90
    salmon, Russian 79
pike 119-20
    dumplings in herb sauce 76
pike-perch 121-2
    baked 77
    fillets, grilled 93
    in a salt crust 78
plaice 114
    brochettes, with scampi 95
    fillets, on brown rice 50
      'Tre Verde' 70
    rolls in green peppers 29
    spring 54
poaching 10
Polish-style Carp 74
pollack 112
pollan 120
polyunsaturates 7
porbeagle shark 115-16
portions 7
potato(es):
    & fish salad, Dutch 106
    fish cakes with 89
    fish soup with 22
    Jansson's Temptation 60
powan 118
prawn(s) 122
    cocktail 35
    curried 47
    king, in garlic butter 39
preparing fresh fish 7, 8-9
protein 7

R

rainbow trout 119
ray 117
red bream 115
redfish 113
    bake, with tomato 56
    baked 64
    Chinese Fish & Rice 65
    fillet, Florentine 44
      with bean sprouts 30
    Fish Roulade 61
    Solyanka 20
red gurnard 116
red mullet 117

Index

red sauce, bass in 33
Rémoulade sauce 108
rice:
  brown, plaice fillets on 50
  Chinese Fish & Rice 65

  risotto, mussel 61
  salad with fish 105
  shrimp salad with 104
risotto *see* rice
rollmops 110
roulade, fish 61
round fish, filleting 8

s

salads 103-7
salmon 120
  flan with cheese 92
  Gravad Lax 36
  mousse, special 38
  pie, Russian 79
  poached, with caviar
    sauce 76
  soufflé with millet 30
  soup, cream 22
  see also smoked salmon
salmon trout 119
salt crust, pike-perch in 78
Salt Herrings with Oatmeal 97
sardine 111

  Mixed Grill 96
sauces:
  Beurre Blanc 108
  caper, halibut steaks in 48
  caviar, poached salmon
    with 76
  cream, mussel ragoût in 52
    with white wine 108
  dill, shrimps in 52
  herb, fish rolls in 45
    pike dumplings in 76
  Hollandaise 108
  horseradish, smoked trout
    with 36
  red, bass in 33
  Rémoulade 108
  tomato, fish rolls in 49
    mussels in 84
  wine, cod in 55

scaling fish 8
scallops 125
  au gratin 39
  Mexican 85
scampi 122
  au gratin with cucumber 31
  brochettes, with plaice 95
  Chinese deep-fried 73
  eating 15

  flambéed 73
  soup, cream, with chives 19
sea fish 110-17
  on a bed of vegetables 57
sea swallow 116
shad 110
shark, porbeagle 115-16
shellfish 7
shopping tips 7
shrimp(s) 122
  cocktail 35
  cucumber &
    dill soup with 19
  in dill sauce 52
  omelettes 29
  pea soup with 24
  peeling 52
  ragoût, vol-au-vents
    with 31
  salad, with cucumber 104
    with rice 104
  Spring Cocktail 34
skate 117
skinning fish 8
smelt 121
smoked fish:
  bean salad with 105
  mousses 82
  with tofu & herb
mayonnaise 83
smoked salmon:
  avocados, stuffed 34
  cream spread 26
  dumplings 21
  rolls, stuffed 27
smooth Venus 125
snacks, special 28
sole 114-15
  eating 15
  fillets 'Tre Verde' 70
  fried, with fine vegetables 70
  stuffed rolled 57
  see also lemon sole
Solyanka 20
soufflé, fish, with millet 30
soups:
  barley, with fish 23
  Bouillabaisse 63
  clear, with dumplings 21

consommé,
  French 25
crayfish 18
cucumber & dill,
  with shrimp 19
dill 21
fish, Chinese 20
  cream of 23
  Spanish 25
  with potatoes 22
mussel, cream of 24
pea, with shrimps 24
salmon, cream of 22
scampi, cream of 19
Solyanka 20
vegetable 21
Soused Herring 100
soy sauce 20
Spanish Fish Soup 25
spinach:
  & cod flan 92
  coley with 34
  fish fillet Florentine 44
  Oysters Rockefeller 40
spiny cockles 124-5
spiny lobster 123
  tails with melon 37
sprat 111
Spring Cocktail 34
spur dog 115-16
squid 123
  with tomatoes 46
steaming 10
sterlet 121
stew, fish & mussel 58
stock, fish 7
stockfish 112
sturgeon 121
  in aspic 81
Swedish Pickled Herring 97
Sweet & Sour Fish 33
swordfish 117

T

tarragon broth, cod cutlets in
  102
tench 121
Terrine of Trout 80
thornback ray 117
toasts, bloater 28

tofu:
  & fish with courgettes 101
  halibut & vegetable

  brochettes with 95
  mayonnaise, with herbs 83
tomato(es):
  & redfish bake 56
  coley with 67
  pan-fried mackerel
    with 54
  sauce, fish rolls in 49
    mussels in 84
  squid with 46
trout 119
  au bleu 51
  in bacon 72
  mousse 82
  pan-fried 51
  pâté en croute 91
  smoked, with horseradish
    sauce 36
  terrine 80
tuna 113
turbot 115
  Sweet & Sour Fish 33

V

vegetable(s):
  & fish in aspic
  mackerel
    with 101
  seafish on 57
  sole with 70
  soup with
    smoked salmon
      dumplings 21
Venus shell 125
Vol-au-vents with Shrimp
  Ragoût 31

W

warty Venus 125
Waterzooi 59
weever 116
white halibut 114
whiting 112-13

wine:
  Burgundy, herrings in 98
  sauce, cod in 56
  white, & cream sauce 108
    Matelote 60
wolf fish *see* catfish